SYNAGOGUE OBJECTS

Many of the objects which beautify the synagogue are similar to the items which were in the Holy Temple in ancient Jerusalem.

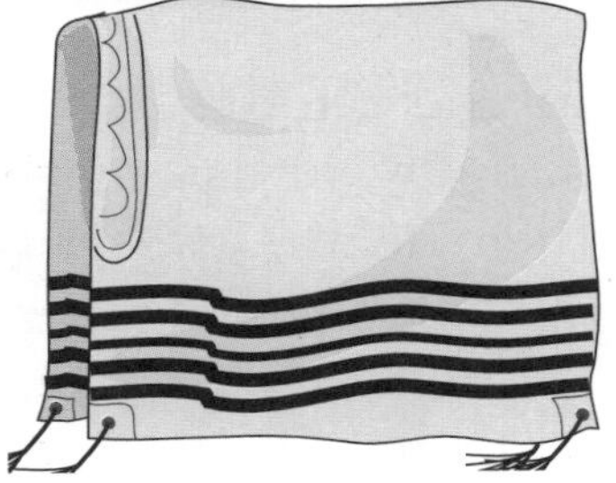

טַלִּית

The טַלִּית is the prayer shawl worn at morning prayers on weekdays, Sabbaths, and festivals. In ancient Israel the rabbis wore a טַלִּית as a sign of distinction. When Jews went to other lands, the טַלִּית came to be used for religious services.

עֲשֶׂרֶת הַדִּבְּרוֹת

In many synagogues an artistic representation of two stone tablets is found on or near the Ark. The ten Hebrew letters on the tablets stand for the עֲשֶׂרֶת הַדִּבְּרוֹת (Ten Commandments).

מְנוֹרָה

The מְנוֹרָה reminds us of the golden seven-branched candelabrum that stood in the Holy Temple. The light it sheds stands for the brightness of the Torah.

סִדּוּר

The סִדּוּר is the prayer book for weekdays and Sabbath. It contains passages from the Bible and from the Talmud as well as selections written by rabbis and poets. The סִדּוּר is mostly in Hebrew, but some of its prayers are in Aramaic.

בִּימָה

The בִּימָה is the raised platform on which the desk stands for the reading of the weekly portion from the Torah and the Prophets. The בִּימָה is often placed in the center of the synagogue, where it represents the altar that once stood in the middle compartment of the Temple.

צְדָקָה

The Temple in Jerusalem had a צְדָקָה box. Contributions were used for Temple repairs and to help the poor. Every synagogue still follows the custom of having a צְדָקָה box, because giving charity is an important מִצְוָה and one of the finest things we can do.

נֵר תָּמִיד

Above the אֲרוֹן קֹדֶשׁ hangs a light which is never permitted to go out. This is the נֵר תָּמִיד ("eternal light"), a symbol of God's continuing presence among us.

PRAYING with SPIRITUALITY

תְּפִלָּה בְּכַוָּנָה

by Sol Scharfstein

illustrated by Dorcas Gelabert

KTAV Publishing House, Inc.

to my
children and grandchildren

may the
Shechinah
always be with them.

Manufactured in the United States of America

ISBN 0-88125-517-3

TABLE OF CONTENTS

THANKS AND ACKNOWLEDGMENTS

To Richard White for his tremendous efforts in bringing this book to its high state of excellence. I appreciate his enthusiastic support and for catching the vision of Tefillah.

To Yaakov Elman for his many thoughtful suggestions.

To Bob Milch for his comments, assistance and erudite editing.

To Howard Adelman an invaluable advisor who has enhanced the text with thoughtful and scholarly comments.

To Lenore Kipper and the Hebrew teachers of Beth Am Day School, Miami, Florida, for their thorough reading of the manuscript and their helpful suggestions.

To June Schwarze for her monumental typing. You did a terrific job.

To my brother Bernie, for giving me the time to dream and for helping me turn my vision into reality.

Responsibility for the content, omissions, decisions and errors rests solely with me.

INTRODUCTION

Tefillah is a second-level Siddur text which follows immediately after a first-level phonics primer. *Tefillah* should be used after the completion of *Haveri I, Leshonee I, Shaar Hakriah I, Reading & Prayer Primer*, or any similar first-level phonics text.

GOALS OF TEFILLAH

Tefillah has been specifically designed to achieve several goals:

1. To improve, speed up, and intensify phonic-reading mastery.
2. To provide historical background to the development of Jewish prayer.
3. To instill a sense of holiness and Kavanah so that prayer can flow from the lips and heart.
4. To illustrate the ethical and moral concepts of Jewish prayer.
5. To familiarize students with the prayer ritual both within the home and in the synagogue.
6. To teach a Hebrew prayer vocabulary.

THE FORMAT

Tefillah is partitioned into two sections: Home Prayers and Shabbat Prayers.

Home Prayer sections include twelve prayers which are customarily recited in the home. The Shabbat Prayer section includes thirteen prayers that are frequently recited during the Saturday morning prayer services.

READING METHODOLOGY

The unique methodology and contents of *Tefillah* make it an ideal teaching tool for any second-level Siddur curriculum. This methodology is based on the successful format of the multi-color edition of *Reading And Prayer Primer*.

Each of the twenty-five prayer modules starts with a two page phonic reading lesson made up of four exercises: Word Endings, Word Beginnings, Word Families and Tefillah Phrases. Each of these four exercises is inter-connected and build upon each other for phonic mastery.

The first exercise, Word Endings, divides long compound poly-syllable words into their shorter root forms and then adds a suffix to produce the regular prayer word. All the Siddur words in that particular prayer with the common suffix are grouped and taught as one phonic unit. The common suffix is printed in red. This phonic repetition produces a rythm reading pattern that speeds up word recognition by reducing the eye fixations. The eye perceives the letters and vowels as blends rather than individual code units.

The same teaching technique is applied to the Word Beginning exercises. Here the emphasis is on prefixes. Once again all words with the same prefixes are grouped together and taught as one unit. All prefixes are printed in red for easier recognition and recall.

The third exercise is entitled Word Families. All words in this prayer with similar roots are grouped together. This type of exercise sensitizes the reader to the grammatical changes which occur in the Hebrew language.

The fourth exercise is entitled Tefillah Phrases. This exercise consists of phrases that the students encounter in the actual prayer. A great many of the words have already been studied and articulated in the previous three sections. This exercise simplifies the transition into the actual prayer.

Now the student is ready to graduate into the actual prayers. Note that all the prayers have been broken down into short phrase segments that make reading easier. All translations are line for line, so that the students can find the meaning for the phrases or individual words.

ALL ABOUT PRAYER

The last section of each module contains explanatory segments, background information, how to function in a synagogue and home, and Kavanah essays.

The explanatory sections of each module bring the prayers into focus and release their history, values, and holy power.

Wherever applicable, How-To information has been included. This type of information familiarizes the students with the prayer ritual and makes the synagogue user friendly.

Each of the modules also contains a Kavanah essay. This essay will stimulate the student's religious response to the fact that prayer is a serious devotion and should not be treated lightly.

In addition, each of the explanatory units features some Hebrew words to increase the student's vocabulary.

The Siddur is a book of Jewish prayer. I want the worshipper to feel at home with its prayers, rituals, and values. I hope that *Tefillah* will start the students on a spiritual journey in their personal quest for the שְׁכִינָה, the Divine Presence.

NOTES:

1. The word יהוה is read Adonai. See page 11.
2. Some grammatical liberties have been taken with the root words in the Word Ending exercises. These deliberate changes were made to simplify the phonic transitions into the siddur words.
3. The aim of the siddur translations is to construct true phrase-by-phrase English readings. However, due to textual difficulties some of the translations have been modified to fit the comprehension rather than the language of the prayer.
4. Some of the English essays have numbers (9) in brackets. These numbers refer to the line numbers in that particular prayer.
5. The vowels patach (ַ)and kametz (ָ)are treated as a single sound.
6. The translations were complicated by trying to make them gender neutral. In most cases I have succeeded without changing the spiritual intention of the prayers. Some of these changes are indicated by the symbol *.attached to the Hebrew word

כַּוָּנָה KAVANAH כַּוָּנָה

THE ANCIENTS

The ancient sages and rabbis were very concerned about how people prayed. They taught that we should not only pray for ourselves but should keep others in mind as we worship. As you study the prayers you will notice that most of them are in the plural form. The rabbis believed that when prayers are unselfish God fulfills the worshipper's request. They said, "All of Israel is responsible for each other." In other words, we are all one large extended family.

The ancients also taught us to pray with feeling. The scholar, Maimonides said, "Turn your thoughts away from everything during Tefillah. When you are engaged in the performance of a religious duty **concentrate** only on what you are doing."

CONCENTRATION

Concentration during prayer is called כַּוָּנָה. If you have true Kavanah your mind is free from other thoughts during prayer, and you are aware that you are standing before the Holy One—God.

When you are in a state of כַּוָּנָה you stop thinking about making plans, arranging meetings, practicing tennis, doing homework, singing, music, taking trips, playing with friends. You stop worrying. You do not have to do anything or go anywhere. Everything is nothing. You are standing before your Creator.

The word כַּוָּנָה comes from the Hebrew word כִּיווּן, meaning "**direction, aim, intention, intonation**". In a religious sense it means **spiritual sincerity**. When you pray with כַּוָּנָה you are opening a direct channel to God. כַּוָּנָה helps you to pray **sincerely**. It is also the power that awakens generosity for the needy,compassion for the poor,and wisdom to use your God-given talents for worthwhile living.

The **spritual sincerity** and unselfish **intention** of Kavanah needs no special time, place or prayer. כַּוָּנָה tells you how to live happily, act wisely, deal generously, and practice friendship.

HOW DO YOU KNOW

How do you know when you have achieved כַּוָּנָה? When you feel really good after praying. When you surprise yourself and say, "Wow, I enjoyed temple services." When you leave the synagogue and sing the tunes out loud. When you do a mitzvah and hadn't even planned to do it. When you stop talking and take the time to recite the food blessings.

GETTING STARTED

There are many ways to start on the road to כַּוָּנָה. Here are a few for starters.

1. Show respect and behave with dignity in the synagogue.
2. Join the prayer service and sing with the congregation. Music intensifies the holy mood of worship.
3. Treat your Siddur and Humash with respect; they are holy books. The Humash contains the words of the Torah, the most sacred book of the Jewish people. The Siddur contains prayers composed by rabbis with special abilities and wisdom implanted by the spirit of God.
4. Learn the meaning and contents of the prayers. When the words of a prayer come out easily without effort, you will be able to concentrate on its spirit.
5. Get involved in congregational activities. Kavanah requires you to be a part of your community and to improve it.
6. Become familiar with the formal procedures and mechanics of the service. Learn when to bow, how to recite the Amidah, when to join in the Kedushah, and more.
7. Free your mind of any distracting thoughts.
8. Concentrate only on the prayers during the service.
9. Jewish law cautions you not to talk, gossip or read other books even the Humash, during prayers.

You can most probably think of other ways to reach the state of כַּוָּנָה. Start by naming one more idea.

תְּפִלּוֹת הַבַּיִת
HOME PRAYERS

תְּפִלּוֹת הַבַּיִת

HOME PRAYERS

Jewish holidays and festivals start in the home and the synagogue, with family. Shabbat starts with candle lighting and Kiddush. Special home ceremonies enliven the holidays of Passover, Rosh Hashanah, Sukkot, Hanukah, and Purim with prayers, beautiful place settings and tasty traditional holiday foods. Jewish living begins in the home, through symbols and religious objects. The highest dramas of Jewish history are reenacted and given new meanings with special prayers and ceremonies.

Celebrating the holidays and experiencing the religious ceremonies and rituals bring the family closer together. When you and your family participate in religious events and ceremonies all of you, become a link in the long chain of Jewish tradition.

This section of the text contains some of the prayers you and your family recite in your home.

BLESSINGS

On these two facing pages you will learn to read some of the words and phrases found in the בְּרָכוֹת.

WORD ENDINGS

1 אֱלֹהִים+נוּ = אֱלֹהֵינוּ   קִדֵּשׁ+נוּ = קִדְּשָׁנוּ,   צִוָּה+נוּ = צִוָּנוּ.

2 צֹרֶךְ+ִי = צָרְכִּי   עָשָׂה+ִי = עָשַׂנִי.

WORD BEGINNINGS

1 הַ+עוֹלָם=הָעוֹלָם   הַ+עֵץ=הָעֵץ,   הַ+מוֹצִיא=הַמּוֹצִיא,

הַ+אֶרֶץ=הָאָרֶץ.

WORD FAMILIES

1 צִוָּנוּ,   מִצְוֹתָיו.

2 עָשָׂה,   עָשַׂנִי.

TEFILLAH PHRASES

1 כָּל-צָרְכִּי,   נֵר שֶׁל שַׁבָּת,   מֶלֶךְ הָעוֹלָם,   קִדְּשָׁנוּ בְּמִצְוֹתָיו.

2 שֶׁעָשַׂנִי יִשְׂרָאֵל,   הַמּוֹצִיא לֶחֶם,   מִן הָאָרֶץ.

3 יוֹם טוֹב,   פְּרִי הָעֵץ,   שֶׁעָשָׂה לִי,   בָּרוּךְ אַתָּה יהוה.

ADONAI יהוה

God's special holy name Adonai was first revealed to Moses at the meeting with God at the burning bush. Moses was shepherding the flock of his father-in-law, Jethro, in the Desert of Sinai. Suddenly, he spied a bush that was aflame, but the bush itself was not consumed by the fire. Adonai called to Moses from the midst of the burning bush and said, "Take off your shoes for the place on which you are standing is holy ground".

God continued and said, "Tell the Children of Israel, that Adonai, the God of your fathers and mothers, spoke to you. This is my name for ever and ever."

God's special divine name is written with four Hebrew letters יהוה, pronounced Adonai. Some non-Jewish scholars pronounced it Yahweh.

It is clear that the four letter Tetragrammaton comes from the Hebrew word הָיָה "to be". It means that God was, God is, and God will forever be.

The secret pronunciation of the name was passed on to Aaron, who passed it on to the High Priest. Whenever the four letter Tetragrammaton יהוה is found in the Bible or Siddur, it is pronounced Adonai. In the Siddur יהוה is sometimes written as יְיָ

BLESSINGS

The Rabbis of the Great Assembly composed a formula for בְּרָכוֹת.
Each בְּרָכָה consists of four parts.
1. The word בָּרוּךְ, meaning "blessed is."
2. God's name, יהוה אֱלֹהֵינוּ.
3. The statement מֶלֶךְ הָעוֹלָם, "Ruler of the World."
4. חֲתִימָה, meaning seal, ends or seals the blessings.

בִּרְכּוֹת הַנֶּהֱנִין

1. Blessed are you, Adonai	1 בָּרוּךְ אַתָּה יהוה
2. Our God, Ruler of the universe,	2 אֱלֹהֵינוּ מֶלֶךְ הָעוֹלָם,
3. Who brings forth bread from the earth.	3 הַמּוֹצִיא לֶחֶם מִן הָאָרֶץ.
4. Blessed are you, Adonai	4 בָּרוּךְ אַתָּה יהוה
5. Our God, Ruler of the universe,	5 אֱלֹהֵינוּ מֶלֶךְ הָעוֹלָם,
6. Who creates the fruit of the tree.	6 בּוֹרֵא פְּרִי הָעֵץ.

בִּרְכּוֹת הַמִּצְוֹת

7. Blessed are you, Adonai	7 בָּרוּךְ אַתָּה יהוה
8. Our God, Ruler of the universe,	8 אֱלֹהֵינוּ מֶלֶךְ הָעוֹלָם,
9. Who has made us holy with Mitzvot	9 אֲשֶׁר קִדְּשָׁנוּ בְּמִצְוֹתָיו,
10. And commanded us to light the Shabbat candle.	10 וְצִוָּנוּ לְהַדְלִיק נֵר שֶׁל שַׁבָּת.
11. Blessed are you, Adonai	11 בָּרוּךְ אַתָּה יהוה
12. Our God, Ruler of the universe,	12 אֱלֹהֵינוּ מֶלֶךְ הָעוֹלָם,
13. Who has made us holy with Mitzvot,	13 אֲשֶׁר קִדְּשָׁנוּ בְּמִצְוֹתָיו,
14. And commanded us to light the holiday candle.	14 וְצִוָּנוּ לְהַדְלִיק נֵר שֶׁל יוֹם טוֹב.

בִּרְכּוֹת הוֹדָאָה

15. Blessed are you, Adonai	15 בָּרוּךְ אַתָּה יהוה
16. Our God, Ruler of the universe,	16 אֱלֹהֵינוּ מֶלֶךְ הָעוֹלָם,
17. Who has made me a Jew.	17 שֶׁעָשַׂנִי יִשְׂרָאֵל.
18. Blessed are you, Adonai	18 בָּרוּךְ אַתָּה יהוה
19. Our God, Ruler of the universe	19 אֱלֹהֵינוּ מֶלֶךְ הָעוֹלָם,
20. Who provides me with all my needs.	20 שֶׁעָשָׂה לִי כָּל-צָרְכִּי.

BLESSINGS בְּרָכוֹת

Of all the wonderful gifts that God has given us, food is most important for life. That is why Jews have made eating a religious act. Many of the blessings we say over food have been grouped together and are together called בִּרְכּוֹת הַנֶהֱנִין, which means "blessings for the enjoyment of various foods." As Jews recite these בְּרָכוֹת, they are linked together as one people all over the world with other Jews saying the same בְּרָכוֹת.

When someone gives you a gift or does you a favor, look him or her in the eye and say, "Thank you." The act of showing appreciation creates a feeling of friendship between giver and receiver. The giver becomes very special. God is a "giver." God has given you a wonderful world and filled it with trees, flowers, all kinds of animals, and marvelous people, as well as you and your family. You are at the receiving end of God's kindness, and when you recite a blessing or a prayer you are thanking the "giver." As you recite a blessing, say the thank you words slowly and with feeling. Remember all your powers and abilities. Give thanks for your gifts. Keep giving thanks.

The Torah tells us that God created a beautiful world filled with clean, swift-running streams, fields of golden grain, gardens green with crunchy vegetables, and orchards with fruit-bearing trees. The rabbis of the Great Assembly wanted us to reach out to God and thank the Creator for all the goodness in the world. So they composed special thank-you blessings for certain foods. The blessings over bread and wine were considered the most important, since these were the basic foods in ancient Israel.

A בְּרָכָה is a blessing. It is a thank-you prayer for a gift from God. The blessings are divided into three groups.

1. בִּרְכּוֹת הַנֶהֱנִין. Blessings to be recited before eating, drinking, or smelling good things such as spices or herbs.
2. בִּרְכּוֹת הַמִּצְוֹת. Blessings to be recited before doing a מִצְוָה, such as lighting Shabbat candles, wrapping oneself in a טַלִּית, or reciting a blessing over the lulav and etrog.
3. בִּרְכּוֹת הוֹדָאָה. Blessings that praise God or ask the creator for something special, such as freedom or good health.

AMEN אָמֵן

The word אָמֵן represents the listener's participation in the reader's recitation of a בְּרָכָה. Some believe the word אָמֵן comes from אֱמוּנָה, meaning "faithfulness." When you answer אָמֵן to someone else's בְּרָכָה, you are participating in thanking God. In addition, it also stands for אֵל מֶלֶךְ נֶאֱמָן, "God is the faithful ruler." The first letters of the preceding three words form the word אָמֵן.

GRACE AFTER MEALS

On these two facing pages you will learn to read some of the words and phrases found in the בִּרְכַּת הַמָּזוֹן.

WORD ENDINGS

1 חֶסֶד+וֹ=חַסְדּוֹ שֵׁם+וֹ=שְׁמוֹ, טוּב+וֹ=טוּבוֹ, שֶׁל+וֹ=שֶׁלוֹ,

כֹּל+וֹ=כֻּלוֹ.

2 אֱלֹהִים+נוּ=אֱלֹהֵינוּ אָכַל+נוּ=אָכַלְנוּ, עַל+נוּ=עָלֵינוּ,

חָיָה+נוּ=חָיִינוּ.

WORD BEGINNINGS

1 ו+בָּרוּךְ=וּבָרוּךְ

ו+בְּטוּבוֹ=וּבְטוּבוֹ, ו+מֵטִיב=וּמֵטִיב,

ו+בְּרַחֲמִים=וּבְרַחֲמִים, ו+מֵכִין=וּמֵכִין.

2 הַ+זָן=הַזָּן

הָ+עוֹלָם=הָעוֹלָם, הַ+גָּדוֹל=הַגָּדוֹל,

הַ+כֹּל=הַכֹּל.

3 לְ+כָל=לְכָל

לְ+עוֹלָם=לְעוֹלָם.

4 בְּ+חֵן=בְּחֵן

בְּ+טוּבוֹ=בְּטוּבוֹ, בְּ+חֶסֶד=בְּחֶסֶד.

WORD FAMILIES

1 בֵּרֵךְ, נְבָרֵךְ, מְבֹרָךְ, בָּרוּךְ.

2 הַזָּן, מָזוֹן, חָסַר, יֶחְסַר.

TEFILLAH PHRASES

1 חֲבֵרַי נְבָרֵךְ, מֵעַתָּה וְעַד עוֹלָם, וּמֵטִיב לַכֹּל.

2 וּבְטוּבוֹ חַיֵּינוּ, הַזָּן אֶת הַכֹּל, הוּא נוֹתֵן לֶחֶם.

3 וּבְטוּבוֹ הַגָּדוֹל, וְאַל יֶחְסַר לָנוּ, שְׁמוֹ הַגָּדוֹל.

4 לְכָל-בָּשָׂר, וּמְפַרְנֵס לַכֹּל.

GRACE AFTER MEALS

When three or more people are present at the meal, a leader is appointed to lead the בִּרְכַּת הַמָּזוֹן. This invitation is called זִמּוּן, from the name of the prayer. The verb זִמֵּן means "to invite." The leader calls on the people at the meal to begin Grace by reciting חֲבֵרַי נְבָרֵךְ ("Friends, let us thank God.")

The leader (מְזַמֵּן) recites:

1. Friends, let us thank God. — 1 חֲבֵרַי נְבָרֵךְ.

The company recites, then the מְזַמֵּן repeats:

2. May Adonai's name be blessed — 2 יְהִי שֵׁם יְיָ מְבֹרָךְ

3. for now and forever. — 3 מֵעַתָּה וְעַד עוֹלָם.

The מְזַמֵּן continues:

4. Friends, with your permission, — 4 בִּרְשׁוּת חֲבֵרַי,

5. We will bless (our God)* whose food we have eaten. — 5 נְבָרֵךְ *(אֱלֹהֵינוּ) שֶׁאָכַלְנוּ מִשֶּׁלּוֹ.

The company responds, then the מְזַמֵּן repeats:

6. We will bless our God, — 6 בָּרוּךְ (אֱלֹהֵינוּ),

7 Whose food we have eaten. — 7 שֶׁאָכַלְנוּ מִשֶּׁלּוֹ*.

8. And by whose goodness we live. — 8 וּבְטוּבוֹ חָיִינוּ.

The מְזַמֵּן recites:

9. Blessed is God, and blessed is the Name. — 9 בָּרוּךְ הוּא וּבָרוּךְ שְׁמוֹ*.

Everyone:

10. Blessed is Adonai — 10 בָּרוּךְ אַתָּה יְיָ

11. Our God, Ruler of the universe, — 11 אֱלֹהֵינוּ מֶלֶךְ הָעוֹלָם,

12. Who feeds the whole world with goodness, — 12 הַזָּן אֶת-הָעוֹלָם כֻּלּוֹ בְּטוּבוֹ,

---

*The word אֱלֹהֵינוּ is added when ten or more are at the table.

13. With love, kindness, and mercy.	13 בְּחֵן בְּחֶסֶד וּבְרַחֲמִים.
14. God provides food for all living things,	14 הוּא נוֹתֵן לֶחֶם לְכָל-בָּשָׂר
15. For God's kindness is forever,	15 כִּי לְעוֹלָם חַסְדּוֹ*.
16. And because of God's great goodness	16 וּבְטוּבוֹ הַגָּדוֹל תָּמִיד,
17. We have never lacked food	17 תָּמִיד לֹא חָסַר לָנוּ,
18. And we will never lack food,	18 וְאַל יֶחְסַר לָנוּ מָזוֹן לְעוֹלָם וָעֶד.
19. For the sake of God's great name.	19 בַּעֲבוּר שְׁמוֹ הַגָּדוֹל;
20. And God feeds and nourishes all living things	20 כִּי הוּא אֵל זָן וּמְפַרְנֵס לַכֹּל
21. And does good for all,	21 וּמֵטִיב לַכֹּל
22. And prepares food	22 וּמֵכִין מָזוֹן
23. For all creatures	23 לְכָל-בְּרִיּוֹתָיו*
24. That God created.	24 אֲשֶׁר בָּרָא.
25. Blessed is Adonai,	25 בָּרוּךְ אַתָּה יהוה,
26 Who feeds everyone.	26 הַזָּן אֶת-הַכֹּל.

BIRKAT HAMAZON בִּרְכַּת הַמָּזוֹן

Before we eat or drink we say a blessing to thank God for giving us food. After we eat and drink we recite בִּרְכַּת הַמָּזוֹן, the Grace after meals, which is made up of beautiful prayers of thanksgiving. We say the בִּרְכַּת הַמָּזוֹן to remind us that even when we are filled with food and satisfied, we must be just as thankful to God as when we were hungry and had just begun to eat.

The Talmud tells us that Moses received the Torah from God and passed it down to Joshua, who passed it on to the prophets, who then handed it on to the Men of the Great Assembly (אַנְשֵׁי כְּנֶסֶת הַגְּדוֹלָה). The Jewish legislative body during the Persian period (500—300 B.C.E.) was called כְּנֶסֶת הַגְּדוֹלָה. It consisted of 120 members who were called into session to make critical decisions. It was the אַנְשֵׁי כְּנֶסֶת הַגְּדוֹלָה that composed most of the prayers and customs in our Siddur as well as the forms of synagogue worship.

Its members determined the format of the בִּרְכַּת הַמָּזוֹן. Included here is a very short version of the בִּרְכַּת הַמָּזוֹן. The longer version includes a prayer for the coming of Elijah and the Messiah. The בִּרְכַּת הַמָּזוֹן ends with a prayer for שָׁלוֹם (peace). The commentator Rashi explains why this prayer was included: "So you have eaten a very tasty and delicious meal, but can you really feel satisfied if there is no שָׁלוֹם?"

Some commentators say that the word חֵן ("kindness") in the Grace refers to food, חֶסֶד to clothing, and רַחֲמִים to a home. All three together provide for a human being's most basic needs, making it possible to lead a happy and normal existence.

God created a beautiful world for humankind. We too must share. We must share God's blessings with those who are less fortunate and not able to support themselves. Thousands of years ago in ancient Israel the poor and the weak were given special rights during the harvest to make sure that they received a share of the crops.

1. They had the rights to anything that grew in the corners of the fields.
2. They had the rights to anything that was accidentally dropped during the harvest.

The Torah tells us that God, in creating the world, provided food for all its creatures. There were special foods for the fish in the seas and oceans, birds in the air, and the animals which roamed the forests and jungles. Above all God created food for the human race. God's kindness, grace, and mercy have provided healthy food for all creatures, human and nonhuman. The sun, the rain, and all of nature's elements are part of a universal food chain which feeds the world's population of people and animals.

WE WILL BLESS נְבָרֵךְ

The Hebrew word נְבָרֵךְ (5) means "we will bless." The rabbis taught that a commandment performed by several people in unison is superior to one done alone. A group reaches a higher degree of holiness than a single person.

The Midrash tells us that Abraham and Sarah were very hospitable. They customarily invited travelers to rest and dine in their tent, and personally served them at the table. After a refreshing meal the traveler would thank his hosts. Abraham and Sarah would reply, בָּרוּךְ אֱלֹהֵינוּ שֶׁאָכַלְנוּ מִשֶּׁלּוֹ ("Thank God whose food we have eaten").

כַּוָּנָה

A teenager once asked her mother, "How do you know that God exists?"

"Well" answered the mother "I've never seen God, but I'm sure there is a God in the world. Let me show you a sample of God's work. Do you see the apple tree in our yard? You've tasted the red apples and enjoyed eating them. Do you remember who planted the tree?"

"Yes," answered the teenager. "I remember taking a tiny seed from an apple, digging a hole in the ground, and burying the seed. And now it has grown into a great big apple tree."

"Now," continued the mother "that one tiny seed, weighing as little as a grain of dust, has grown into a huge tree that keeps on producing delicious apples the exact same time each year.

"It's true that you can't see God, but you can see God's miracles growing all around you.

Judaism believes that the table upon which we eat is an altar and that every meal should be proceeded with a thank-you prayer.

The Kabbalists of the sixteenth century added a touch a joy to the בִּרְכַּת הַמָּזוֹן by singing songs of adoration. These sacred songs are called זְמִירוֹת. They were composed during one of the saddest periods of Jewish history. The mystics felt that the act of singing helped change the mood of sadness to joy.

SABBATH CANDLE LIGHTING

On these two facing pages you will learn to read some of the words and phrases found in the הַדְלָקַת הַנֵּרוֹת שֶׁל שַׁבָּת.

WORD ENDINGS

1 קִדֵּשׁ+נוּ=קִדְּשָׁנוּ   אֱלֹהִים+נוּ=אֱלֹהֵינוּ,   צִוָּה+נוּ=צִוָּנוּ.

2 יָשִׂים+ךָ=יְשִׂימְךָ   יִשְׁמֹר+ךָ=יִשְׁמְרֶךָ,   אֶל+ךָ=אֵלֶיךָ,

יָחֹן+ךָ=יְחֻנֶּךָּ,   יְבָרֵךְ+ךָ=יְבָרֶכְךָ.

3 מִצְוֹת+■ָיו=מִצְוֹתָיו   פָּנִים+■ָיו=פָּנָיו.

WORD BEGINNINGS

1 וְ+כְמְנַשֶּׁה = וְכִמְנַשֶּׁה   וְ+לֵאָה = וְלֵאָה,   וְ+יִשְׁמְרֶךָ = וְיִשְׁמְרֶךָ,
וְ+יָשֵׂם = וְיָשֵׂם,   וְ+צִוָּנוּ = וְצִוָּנוּ.

2 כְּ+אֶפְרַיִם = כְּאֶפְרַיִם   כְּ+שָׂרָה = כְּשָׂרָה.

WORD FAMILIES

1 צִוָּה, צִוָּנוּ, מִצְוֹתָיו.

2 אֱלֹהִים, אֱלֹהֵינוּ.

3 שִׂים, יִשִׂמְךָ, יְשִׂמֵךְ, יָשֵׂם.

4 בֵּרַךְ, בָּרוּךְ, יְבָרֶכְךָ.

TEFILLAH PHRASES

1 מֶלֶךְ הָעוֹלָם,   לְהַדְלִיק נֵר,   שֶׁל שַׁבָּת.

2 יְבָרֶכְךָ יְיָ,   יִשָּׂא יְיָ פָּנָיו אֵלֶיךָ.

3 יָאֵר יְיָ פָּנָיו,   רָחֵל וְלֵאָה,   יְשִׂמֵךְ אֱלֹהִים.

4 אֵלֶיךָ וִיחֻנֶּךָּ,   כְּאֶפְרַיִם וְכִמְנַשֶּׁה,   בָּרוּךְ אַתָּה יהוה.

SABBATH CANDLE LIGHTING

The brightly burning Sabbath candles, the sparkling of red wine, the soft Hallah and a loving family make the שַׁבָּת a "delight."

Candle Lighting הַדְלָקַת הַנֵּרוֹת

1. Blessed are you, Adonai	1 בָּרוּךְ אַתָּה יהוה
2. Our God, Ruler of the universe,	2 אֱלֹהֵינוּ מֶלֶךְ הָעוֹלָם,
3. Who has made us holy with Mitzvot,	3 אֲשֶׁר קִדְּשָׁנוּ בְּמִצְוֹתָיו
4. And commanded us to light the Sabbath candles.	4 וְצִוָּנוּ לְהַדְלִיק נֵר שֶׁל שַׁבָּת.

For a boy: בִּרְכַּת הַבָּנִים

5. May God make you	5 יְשִׂמְךָ אֱלֹהִים
6. Like Ephraim and Manasseh.	6 כְּאֶפְרַיִם וְכִמְנַשֶּׁה.

For a girl: בִּרְכַּת הַבָּנוֹת

7. May God make you	7 יְשִׂמֵךְ אֱלֹהִים
8. Like Sarah, Rebecca, Rachel, and Leah.	8 כְּשָׂרָה, רִבְקָה, רָחֵל, וְלֵאָה.

For all the children:

9. May Adonai bless you and guard you,	9 יְבָרֶכְךָ יְיָ וְיִשְׁמְרֶךָ.
10. May Adonai's face shine upon you,	10 יָאֵר יְיָ פָּנָיו אֵלֶיךָ
11. And be gracious to you,	11 וִיחֻנֶּךָּ.
12. May Adonai's face turn towards you.	12 יִשָּׂא יְיָ פָּנָיו אֵלֶיךָ
13. And grant you peace.	13 וְיָשֵׂם לְךָ שָׁלוֹם.

CHILDREN'S BLESSINGS בִּרְכוֹת הַבָּנִים

Placing a hand on a child's head has become a symbol of transmitting the spirit of God and the love of parents for their children. This ceremony can be performed by the parents together or individually.

People in the family belong to each other. They share and care for each other. Helping and sharing is an important part of the Jewish way of life. You can enjoy youre pleasures and triumphs even more when you share them with your family.

A family is also for sharing troubles. It helps a lot just to discuss your problems with someone you love and who loves you. But, in real life sometimes people in the family get angry with each other and yell and say something stupid. However, the wonderful thing is that in a loving family you quickly forgive and forget.

The בִּרְכַּת הַבָּנִים *is a reminder that you are a valued part of a wonderful family who, like Ephraim and Manasseh, have chosen the Jewish way of life. You are an important member of your family. Help your parents in any way to show them how glad and grateful you are for their loving care. By caring you will help to make your family a happy one. You also will be living up to the Fifth Commandment that says, "Honor your father, and your mother."*

As the patriarch Jacob lay dying, he blessed Joseph's children, Ephraim and Manasseh. He said to Joseph, "Now the sons who were born to you in Egypt before I came here shall be considered as mine. Ephraim and Manasseh shall be on an equal level with Reuben and Simeon." . . . "In time to come the people of Israel will use you as a blessing. They will say, 'May God make you like Ephraim and Manasseh'." Ephraim and Manasseh willingly gave up the riches of the palace and a high position in Egypt, and openly identified themselves with the Jews.

Before the invention of clocks it was difficult to determine the exact time to light the שַׁבָּת candles. In ancient Israel, six blasts were blown on a trumpet on Friday afternoon before sunset. The third blast alerted the population to light the שַׁבָּת candles. Today most Jewish calendars list the time for lighting the candles on the שַׁבָּת.

Just as creation began on the first day with the words "Let there be light," so the celebration of שַׁבָּת begins with the lighting of the candles. The שַׁבָּת atmosphere is created in the home by the lighting of the candles. Women usually light the candles. However, men can also participate in the מִצְוָה of candle lighting. Customs vary as to the number of candles to be lighted. Some families start with two and add an additional candle for each child.

Usually blessings are recited before the act they sanctify. The בְּרָכָה for the Sabbath candles, however, is recited after they have been lit. The person who recites the benediction closes his or her eyes while doing so. Some say that covering the eyes prevents distractions of the mind and thus increases one's Kavanah (concentration) while saying the blessing. Candles are also lighted on holidays and festivals. The brightly burning candles create an atmosphere filled with love, peace, and family harmony.

KIDDUSH FOR FRIDAY EVENING

On these two facing pages you will learn to read some of the words and phrases found in the קִדּוּשׁ.

WORD ENDINGS

1 אֶת+וֹ=אֹתוֹ — מְלָאכָה+וֹ=מְלַאכְתּוֹ, קֹדֶשׁ+וֹ=קָדְשׁוֹ.

2 אֱלֹהִים+נוּ=אֱלֹהֵינוּ — הִנְחִיל+נוּ=הִנְחִילָנוּ, אֶת+נוּ=אוֹתָנוּ,

קִדֵּשׁ+נוּ=קִדְּשָׁנוּ, בְּ+נוּ=בָּנוּ,

הִנְחַלְתָּ+נוּ=הִנְחַלְתָּנוּ.

3 בָּחַר+תָּ=בָּחַרְתָּ — קִדֵּשׁ+תָּ=קִדַּשְׁתָּ.

4 שֵׁשׁ+■ִי=שִׁשִּׁי — שֶׁבַע+■ִי=שְׁבִיעִי.

WORD BEGINNINGS

1 הַ + שִּׁשִּׁי = הַשִּׁשִּׁי הַ + שָׁמַיִם = הַשָּׁמַיִם, הָ + אֶרֶץ = הָאָרֶץ,

הַ + שְׁבִיעִי = הַשְּׁבִיעִי, הָ + עוֹלָם = הָעוֹלָם,

הָ + עַמִּים = הָעַמִּים, הַ + שַׁבָּת = הַשַּׁבָּת.

2 וַ + יְבָרֶךְ = וַיְבָרֶךְ וַ + יְכֻלּוּ = וַיְכֻלּוּ, וַ + יְקַדֵּשׁ = וַיְקַדֵּשׁ,

3 וְ + רָצָה = וְרָצָה וְ + כָל = וְכָל, וְ + רַבּוֹתַי = וְרַבּוֹתַי,

וְ + שַׁבַּת = וְשַׁבַּת, וְ + אוֹתָנוּ = וְאוֹתָנוּ.

4 בְּ + מִצְוֹתָיו = בְּמִצְוֹתָיו בְּ + אַהֲבָה = בְּאַהֲבָה.

WORD FAMILIES

1 שָׁבַת, יִשְׁבֹּת, שַׁבַּת, הַשַּׁבָּת.

2 קֹדֶשׁ, יְקַדֵּשׁ, קָדְשְׁךָ, מְקַדֵּשׁ.

TEFILLAH PHRASES

1 יוֹם הַשִּׁשִּׁי, הַמּוֹצִיא לֶחֶם, וְרָצָה בָנוּ, בְּאַהֲבָה וּבְרָצוֹן.

2 בַּיּוֹם הַשְּׁבִיעִי, וְשַׁבַּת קָדְשׁוֹ, כִּי בָנוּ בָחַרְתָּ, מִכָּל הָעַמִּים.

3 מִכָּל מְלַאכְתּוֹ, קִדְּשָׁנוּ בְּמִצְוֹתָיו, לְמַעֲשֵׂה בְרֵאשִׁית.

4 מְקַדֵּשׁ הַשַּׁבָּת, וַיְכֻלּוּ הַשָּׁמַיִם, וְאוֹתָנוּ קִדַּשְׁתָּ, אֲשֶׁר עָשָׂה.

KIDDUSH FOR FRIDAY EVENING

קִדּוּשׁ means "sanctification" or "making holy."

The Friday night קִדּוּשׁ is from the first book of the Torah, Genesis 2:1–3.

1. It was evening and it was morning,	1 וַיְהִי-עֶרֶב וַיְהִי-בֹקֶר
2. On the sixth day,	2 יוֹם הַשִּׁשִּׁי:
3. When the heavens were finished,	3 וַיְכֻלּוּ הַשָּׁמַיִם,
4. The earth and everything in them,	4 וְהָאָרֶץ וְכָל-צְבָאָם,
5. And on the seventh day God completed,	5 וַיְכַל אֱלֹהִים בַּיּוֹם הַשְּׁבִיעִי,
6. The work of creation,	6 מְלַאכְתּוֹ* אֲשֶׁר עָשָׂה:
7. And God rested on the seventh day,	7 וַיִּשְׁבֹּת בַּיּוֹם הַשְּׁבִיעִי,
8. From doing all the work of creation.	8 מִכָּל מְלַאכְתּוֹ אֲשֶׁר עָשָׂה.
9. And God blessed the seventh day	9 וַיְבָרֶךְ אֱלֹהִים אֶת יוֹם הַשְּׁבִיעִי
10. And made it holy,	10 וַיְקַדֵּשׁ אֹתוֹ,
11. Because on that day God rested from all labor,	11 כִּי בוֹ שָׁבַת מִכָּל מְלַאכְתּוֹ
12. Which God had created and made,	12 אֲשֶׁר בָּרָא אֱלֹהִים לַעֲשׂוֹת.
	13 סַבְרִי מָרָנָן וְרַבּוֹתַי:

On wine:

17. Blessed are you, Adonai	14 בָּרוּךְ אַתָּה יְיָ,
18. Our God, Ruler of the universe,	15 אֱלֹהֵינוּ מֶלֶךְ הָעוֹלָם,
19. Who created the fruit of the vine.	16 בּוֹרֵא פְּרִי הַגָּפֶן.

On hallah:

14. Blessed are you, Adonai	17 בָּרוּךְ אַתָּה יְיָ,
15. Our God, Ruler of the universe,	18 אֱלֹהֵינוּ מֶלֶךְ הָעוֹלָם,
16. Who brings forth bread from the earth.	19 הַמּוֹצִיא לֶחֶם מִן הָאָרֶץ.

20. Blessed are you, Adonai,	20 בָּרוּךְ אַתָּה יְיָ,
21. Our God, Ruler of the universe,	21 אֱלֹהֵינוּ מֶלֶךְ הָעוֹלָם,
22. Who made us holy with Mitzvot	22 אֲשֶׁר קִדְּשָׁנוּ בְּמִצְוֹתָיו*
23. And was pleased with us.	23 וְרָצָה בָנוּ.
24. And God's holy Shabbat,	24 וְשַׁבַּת קָדְשׁוֹ,
25. With love and pleasure has been given to us,	25 בְּאַהֲבָה וּבְרָצוֹן הִנְחִילָנוּ,
26. A reminder of the creation.	26 זִכָּרוֹן לְמַעֲשֵׂה בְרֵאשִׁית.
27. For this day,	27 כִּי הוּא יוֹם,
28. Is the first of the holy festivals,	28 תְּחִלָּה לְמִקְרָאֵי קֹדֶשׁ,
29. A reminder of the exodus from Egypt.	29 זֵכֶר לִיצִיאַת מִצְרָיִם.
30. For you have chosen us,	30 כִּי בָנוּ בָחַרְתָּ,
31. And you made us holy among all peoples.	31 וְאוֹתָנוּ קִדַּשְׁתָּ מִכָּל הָעַמִּים.
32. And Your holy Shabbat,	32 וְשַׁבַּת קָדְשְׁךָ,
33. With love and pleasure is our inheritance.	33 בְּאַהֲבָה וּבְרָצוֹן הִנְחַלְתָּנוּ.
34. Blessed are you, Adonai,	34 בָּרוּךְ אַתָּה יְיָ,
35. Who makes Shabbat holy.	35 מְקַדֵּשׁ הַשַּׁבָּת.

The rabbis in the Talmud considered that wine drunk in moderation gladdens the heart.

The Aramaic phrase סַבְרִי מָרָנָן וְרַבּוֹתַי was inserted into the קִדּוּשׁ to alert the people to stand and listen to the blessings. The words mean "with the permission of those present."

Wine is an important part of many of our religious ceremonies. The קִדּוּשׁ and the סֵדֶר are conducted with wine. Four cups of wine are drunk at the seder, two cups of wine at a wedding ceremony, and one at a circumcision.

With the beginning of the modern Jewish settlements in Palestine in 1882, the first vineyards were planted at Rishon Le-Zion. Baron Edmond de Rothschild brought specialists from France to help produce high-quality wine. He helped build large cellars to store the wine. Today the modern State of Israel has a highly developed wine industry. It produces and sells millions of bottles of medal-winning wines all over the world.

When wine is not available the קִדּוּשׁ is recited over two loaves of bread. The two loaves are in memory of the double portion of manna that was gathered by the Israelites in the desert on Fridays.

The קִדּוּשׁ reminds us of two reasons given in the Torah for observing the Shabbat:

1. Because God rested on the seventh day.
2. Because we were brought out of Egypt and freed from slavery. A slave has no choice but to work seven days a week. We are not slaves. We can rest on the Shabbat.

The mitzvah of hospitality—הַכְנָסַת אוֹרְחִים—is prominent in the Bible and Talmud. For example, Abraham and Sarah welcomed three strangers into their tent and provided them with food and water. In Ethics Of The Fathers, an ancient sage says, "Let your house be open, treat the poor as members of your family".

Years ago, in the small towns of Europe and other parts of the world, there were no hotels or motels at which Jewish travelers could stop and spend the שַׁבָּת. The synagogue provided the הַכְנָסַת אוֹרְחִים for the weary traveler. They set aside a room and shared their food with the travellers.

At first, the Friday night קִדּוּשׁ was recited only in the home. But, for the sake of the Jewish travelers who spent the שַׁבָּת in the synagogue, קִדּוּשׁ began to be recited there as well.

You too can practice the mizvah of הַכְנָסַת אוֹרְחִים by welcoming the new kids in your class or in your neighborhood. All people need to feel welcome and you can encourage them to feel at home by performing the mitzvah of הַכְנָסַת אוֹרְחִים.

TEFILAH תְּפִלָּה

The Jewish religion has a set time for prayers—a schedule of occasions, seasons, holidays, and times which a person should set aside as a time to pray. During the week, our religious leaders ordained three religious services: שַׁחֲרִית (the morning prayer), מִנְחָה (the afternoon prayer), and מַעֲרִיב (the evening prayer). The Talmud provides several reasons for these three divisions.

1. The day is divided into three natural divisions: morning, afternoon, and night.
2. The three patriarchs: Abraham prayed in the morning, Isaac in the afternoon, and Jacob at night.
3. There were three daily offerings and prayer sessions in the ancient Temple in Jerusalem: morning, afternoon, and night.

KIDDUSH קִדּוּשׁ

The initials of the first four words in the Kiddush יוֹם הַשִּׁשִּׁי וַיְכֻלּוּ הַשָּׁמַיִם form the holy name of God. י-ה-ו-ה

SIDDUR סִדּוּר

The word סִדּוּר means "order." The Jewish prayerbook is called a סִדּוּר because it contains the daily, Sabbath, and holiday prayers in their special order and rotation.

Many of the prayers, such as the קִדּוּשׁ and the Psalms, come from the Tanach (Bible). Some of the other prayers were composed by rabbis, poets, and scholars.The first complete סִדּוּר was arranged in the ninth century by Rabbi Amram of the Great Academy in Babylonia. He arranged the order of the prayers for various occasions and prescribed the rules for synagogue and home worship. This served as the basis of later סִדּוּר arrangements.

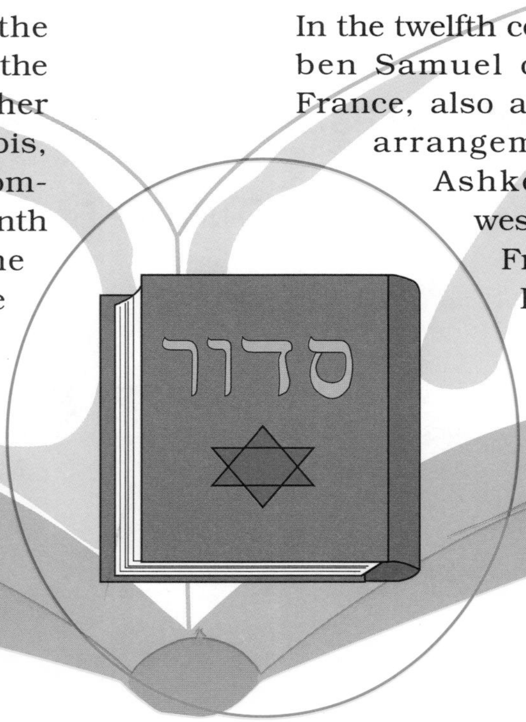

In the twelfth century, Rabbi Simcha ben Samuel of Vitry, a town in France, also arranged a סִדּוּר. His arrangement reflected the Ashkenazi Jews of the western lands: England, France, Germany, and Russia. It is now widely used by Ashkenazi Jews in North America.

KIDDUSH FOR THE FESTIVALS

On these two facing pages you will learn to read some of the words and phrases found in the
קִדּוּשׁ לְשָׁלֹשׁ רְגָלִים.

WORD ENDINGS

1 אֱלֹהִם+נוּ=אֱלֹהֵינוּ
וְרוֹמֵם+נוּ=וְרוֹמְמָנוּ, הִנְחַלְתָּ+נוּ=הִנְחַלְתָּנוּ.

2 חֵרוּת+נוּ=חֵרוּתֵנוּ
תּוֹרָה+נוּ=תּוֹרָתֵנוּ, שִׂמְחָה+נוּ=שִׂמְחָתֵנוּ,
אֶת+נוּ=אוֹתָנוּ, קִדֵּשׁ+נוּ=קִדְּשָׁנוּ.

3 זְמַן+■ִים=זְמַנִּים
מוֹעֵד+■ִים=מוֹעֲדִים, עַם+ִּים=עַמִּים

4 שָׁבֻעַ+וֹת=שָׁבֻעוֹת
סֻכָּה+וֹת=סֻכּוֹת, מַצָּה+וֹת=מַצּוֹת,
שַׁבָּת+וֹת=שַׁבָּתוֹת.

5 בָּחַר+תָּ=בָּחַרְתָּ
קִדֵּשׁ+תָּ=קִדַּשְׁתָּ.

WORD BEGINNING

1 וַ+יְהִי=וַיְהִי   וַ+יְכֻלּוּ=וַיְכֻלּוּ,   וַ+יְבָרֵךְ=וַיְבָרֵךְ,

וַ+יְקַדֵּשׁ=וַיְקַדֵּשׁ.

2 וּ+מוֹעֲדֵי=וּמוֹעֲדֵי   וּ+בְרָצוֹן=וּבְרָצוֹן,   וּ+מוֹעֲדִים=וּמוֹעֲדִים.

3 בְּ+רָצוֹן=בְּרָצוֹן   בְּ+שִׂמְחָה=בְּשִׂמְחָה,   בְּ+שָׂשׂוֹן=בְּשָׂשׂוֹן,

בְּ+אַהֲבָה=בְּאַהֲבָה,   בְּ+מִצְוֹתָיו=בְּמִצְוֹתָיו.

4 לְ+שִׂמְחָה=לְשִׂמְחָה   לְ+שָׂשׂוֹן=לְשָׂשׂוֹן.

5 וְ+שַׁבָּת=וְשַׁבָּת   וְ+הַזְּמַנִּים=וְהַזְּמַנִּים,   וְ+יִשְׂרָאֵל=וְיִשְׂרָאֵל,

וְ+קִדְּשָׁנוּ=וְקִדְּשָׁנוּ,   וְ+כָל=וְכָל,

וְ+רוֹמְמָנוּ, =וְרוֹמְמָנוּ,   וְ+אוֹתָנוּ=וְאוֹתָנוּ.

6 הַ+סֻּכּוֹת=הַסֻּכּוֹת   הַ-זֶה=הַזֶּה,   הַ+מַּצּוֹת=הַמַּצּוֹת,

הַ+שְּׁמִינִי=הַשְּׁמִינִי,   הַ+עֲצֶרֶת=הָעֲצֶרֶת,

הָ+עוֹלָם=הָעוֹלָם,   הַ+עַמִּים=הָעַמִּים,

הַ+שַּׁבָּת=הַשַּׁבָּת,   הַ+שָּׁבֻעוֹת=הַשָּׁבֻעוֹת,

הַ+שָּׁמַיִם=הַשָּׁמַיִם,   הַ+אֶרֶץ=הָאָרֶץ.

TEFILLAH PHRASES

1 מוֹעֲדֵי קָדְשֶׁךָ,   יִשְׂרָאֵל וְהַזְּמַנִּים,   יוֹם הַשִּׁשִּׁי, מִקְרָא קֹדֶשׁ.

2 בְּאַהֲבָה וּבְרָצוֹן,   וַיְכֻלּוּ הַשָּׁמַיִם,   וְרוֹמְמָנוּ מִכָּל לָשׁוֹן, וַיְהִי בֹקֶר.

3 בְּשִׂמְחָה וּבְשָׂשׂוֹן,   בַּיּוֹם הַשְּׁבִיעִי,   זְמַן חֵרוּתֵנוּ, חַג הַשָּׁבֻעוֹת.

KIDDUSH FOR FESTIVALS

A special form of קִדּוּשׁ is recited in the home and in the synagogue on most Jewish holidays. The following קִדּוּשׁ is recited on Passover, Shavuot, Sukkot, and Shemini Atzeret.

On Friday night start here:

1. It was evening and it was morning,	1 וַיְהִי עֶרֶב וַיְהִי בֹקֶר,
2. On the sixth day.	2 יוֹם הַשִּׁשִּׁי.
3. And when the heavens were finished,	3 וַיְכֻלּוּ הַשָּׁמַיִם,
4. And the earth and everything in them,	4 וְהָאָרֶץ וְכָל צְבָאָם,
5. And on the seventh day God completed,	5 וַיְכַל אֱלֹהִים בַּיּוֹם הַשְּׁבִיעִי,
6. The work of creation.	6 מְלַאכְתּוֹ* אֲשֶׁר עָשָׂה.
7. And God rested on the seventh day,	7 וַיִּשְׁבֹּת בַּיּוֹם הַשְּׁבִיעִי
8. From doing all the work of creation,	8 מִכָּל מְלַאכְתּוֹ אֲשֶׁר עָשָׂה.
9. And God blessed the seventh day	9 וַיְבָרֶךְ אֱלֹהִים אֶת יוֹם הַשְּׁבִיעִי
10. And made it holy,	10 וַיְקַדֵּשׁ אֹתוֹ,
11. Because on that day God rested from all labor,	11 כִּי בוֹ שָׁבַת מִכָּל מְלַאכְתּוֹ,
12. Which God had created and made,	12 אֲשֶׁר בָּרָא אֱלֹהִים לַעֲשׂוֹת,

On weekdays start here:

13 סַבְרִי מָרָנָן וְרַבּוֹתַי:

On wine:

17. Blessed are you, Adonai,	14 בָּרוּךְ אַתָּה יְיָ,
18. Our God, Ruler of the universe,	15 אֱלֹהֵינוּ מֶלֶךְ הָעוֹלָם,
19. Who created the fruit of the vine.	16 בּוֹרֵא פְּרִי הַגָּפֶן.

On hallah:

14. Blessed are you, Adonai,	17 בָּרוּךְ אַתָּה יְיָ,
15. Our God, Ruler of the universe,	18 אֱלֹהֵינוּ מֶלֶךְ הָעוֹלָם,
16. Who brings forth bread from the earth.	19 הַמּוֹצִיא לֶחֶם מִן הָאָרֶץ.

20. Blessed are you, Adonai, 20 בָּרוּךְ אַתָּה יְיָ,

21. Our God, Ruler of the universe, 21 אֱלֹהֵינוּ מֶלֶךְ הָעוֹלָם,

22. Who has chosen us from among all nations, 22 אֲשֶׁר בָּחַר בָּנוּ מִכָּל עָם,

23. And raised us above all other peoples, 23 וְרוֹמְמָנוּ מִכָּל לָשׁוֹן,

24. And made us holy with Mitzvot. 24 וְקִדְּשָׁנוּ בְּמִצְוֹתָיו.

25. And in love have given us 25 וַתִּתֶּן לָנוּ יְיָ אֱלֹהֵינוּ בְּאַהֲבָה

26. (Shabbats for rest and) Festivals for joy, 26 (שַׁבָּתוֹת לִמְנוּחָה וּ)מוֹעֲדִים לְשִׂמְחָה,

27. Holidays and seasons for happiness 27 חַגִּים וּזְמַנִּים לְשָׂשׂוֹן

28. This day of (Shabbat and the day of) 28 אֶת יוֹם (הַשַּׁבָּת הַזֶּה וְאֶת יוֹם)

On Passover:

29. The Festival of Matzot, our season of freedom; 29 חַג הַמַּצּוֹת הַזֶּה, זְמַן חֵרוּתֵנוּ;

On Shavuot:

30. The Festival of Shavuot, 30 חַג הַשָּׁבֻעוֹת הַזֶּה,

31. The season of the giving of our Torah; 31 זְמַן מַתַּן תּוֹרָתֵנוּ;

On Sukkot:

32. This Festival of Sukkot, the season of our joy; 32 חַג הַסֻּכּוֹת הַזֶּה, זְמַן שִׂמְחָתֵנוּ;

On Shemini Atzeret and Simhat Torah:

33. The Festival of Shemini Atzeret, 33 הַשְּׁמִינִי חַג הָעֲצֶרֶת הַזֶּה,

34. The season of our rejoicing; 34 זְמַן שִׂמְחָתֵנוּ;

35. (With love) On Shabbat 35 (בְּאַהֲבָה)

36. A day of holy assembly, 36 מִקְרָא קֹדֶשׁ

37. And memory of the Exodus from Egypt, 37 זֵכֶר לִיצִיאַת מִצְרָיִם,

37. Because You have chosen us 38 כִּי בָנוּ בָחַרְתָּ

38. And made us holier than all the nations. 39 וְאוֹתָנוּ קִדַּשְׁתָּ מִכָּל הָעַמִּים,

39. And You appointed (Shabbat and) Festivals of Holiness 40 (וְשַׁבָּת) וּמוֹעֲדֵי קָדְשֶׁךָ

40. (With love and pleasure) 41 (בְּאַהֲבָה וּבְרָצוֹן)

41. With joy and happiness You gave us a inheritance. 42 בְּשִׂמְחָה וּבְשָׂשׂוֹן הִנְחַלְתָּנוּ.

42. Blessed are You, Adonai, 43 בָּרוּךְ אַתָּה יְיָ,

43. Who makes (Shabbat and) Israel and the Festivals of Holiness. 44 מְקַדֵּשׁ (הַשַּׁבָּת וְ)יִשְׂרָאֵל וְהַזְּמַנִּים.

THE THREE FESTIVALS שָׁלוֹשׁ רְגָלִים

The שָׁלוֹשׁ רְגָלִים are the three pilgrimage festivals. These three holidays were originally agricultural in nature. Pesach marked the spring barley harvest in Israel. Shavuot commemorated the summer wheat harvest. Sukkot celebrated the autumn harvest in the Holy Land. During these three pilgrimage seasons, the Israelites would march with song and dance from all four corners of the land to the Holy Temple in Jerusalem. On Shavuot, for example, each farmer carried a portion of the first fruits of his harvest as a thank-you gift to God. They wanted to thank God for sending rain to water the crops and the sun to warm them and make them grow. The word שָׁלוֹשׁ means "three." According to Rabbi Ibn Ezra, the word רְגָלִים comes from the custom of "marching on foot" (רֶגֶל). Thus the holidays became known as the holidays of שָׁלוֹשׁ רְגָלִים.

SUKKOT סֻכּוֹת

In the Bible, סֻכּוֹת has two names:
1) חַג הָאָסִיף: Festival of Ingathering. 2) סֻכּוֹת: Festival of Booths. After our ancestors left Egypt, the Torah tells us, they wandered for forty years in the desert before they reached the Promised Land. During all these years they lived in makeshift shelters called סֻכּוֹת, made of dry palm branches. The Torah tells us to dwell in סֻכּוֹת seven days each year in remembrance of the years of wandering and hardship. After our ancestors had settled in Canaan, they discovered that the autumn, when סֻכּוֹת was celebrated, was also the time to gather in the crops. So סֻכּוֹת became a double celebration.

סֻכּוֹת is also known as חַג הָאָסִיף, the Harvest Festival. At this time the fruit harvest was finished. The grapes were ready to be pressed into wine and the olives to be pressed into oil.

PASSOVER פֶּסַח

Passover is many things. One is a Festival of Freedom, when we recall how God rescued our ancestors from slavery in Egypt.

פֶּסַח is an agricultural festival, reminding us of the Land of Israel in the time of the First and Second Temples. In those days, our ancestors were farmers tilling the soil for a livelihood. Passover marked the beginning of the wheat harvest. פֶּסַח is also a Pilgrim Festival. Three times during the year, the Israelites, according to the laws of the Torah, went in joyous pilgrimage to Jerusalem to celebrate the festivals of פֶּסַח, שָׁבֻעוֹת, and סֻכּוֹת. Passover is all these things, but it is especially a holiday for children. Out ancestors were instructed: "You shall tell it to your children." The Seder Service, the reading of the Haggadah, the Four Questions, the Kiddush, the "stealing of the afikomen"—all these are meant for boys and girls, to teach them the importance of this great holiday in the history of the Jewish people.

The Haggadah is a kind of "guide book" for the celebration of פֶּסַח. It has directions on how to conduct the Seder, explanations for the פֶּסַח symbols, interesting stories, children's folk songs, riddles and prayers. Most important of all, it tells the story of why we celebrate פֶּסַח.

SHAVUOT שָׁבֻעוֹת

שָׁבֻעוֹת is the third of the שָׁלוֹשׁ רְגָלִים, the three pilgrimage festivals on which Jews from all parts of Israel used to make pilgrimages to the Holy Temple in Jerusalem. שָׁבֻעוֹת means "weeks." This festival falls exactly seven weeks after the second day of Passover.

As a Torah festival שָׁבֻעוֹת is known as זְמַן מַתַּן תּוֹרָתֵנוּ. This means "the time of the giving of our Torah." It was on שָׁבֻעוֹת that God spoke to Moses on top of Mount Sinai and gave him the Ten Commandments.

Besides being a Torah festival, שָׁבֻעוֹת is also a harvest festival.In ancient days the grain-harvest was begun on the second day of Passover with the ripening of the barley. On this day an עֹמֶר (measure) of grain was brought to the Temple as a thank-you gift to God.

Because the Jewish people received the Torah on שָׁבֻעוֹת, it is also the holiday for a special ceremony in which men and women are confirmed. Youngsters who have completed the course of study in a religious school become confirmed and are initiated into the fellowship of the Jewish people.

Each day of the forty-nine days from Passover till שָׁבֻעוֹת was counted day by day, and this period is still called the Counting of the Omer. Along with the count, a special prayer was, and still is, recited each day at the end of the evening service in traditional homes and synagogues. After seven weeks of counting came the harvest of wheat, the last grain to ripen. Thus שָׁבֻעוֹת is also know as חַג הַקָּצִיר ("the harvest festival").

When the Israelites entered Canaan, they were a group of individual tribes concerned only with their own piece of territory. The building of the Holy Temple in Jerusalem helped mold these individual tribes into a strong united nation.

Three times a year, on Sukkot, Passover, and Shavout, the Jews marched on a pilgrimage from all four corners of the kingdom to the Holy Temple. The farmers and shepherds brought the best of their crops and animals as a gift for the needy. At the Temple Israelites from all tribes prayed as one nation, sang as one choir, and studied Torah as one large class.

Today, wherever there are a number of Jews, there is a miniature Temple called the synagogue. On Shabbat, on Jewish holidays, and on special occasions, entire families pilgrimage to the synagogue to pray and sing and study as one large, united people.

Raise your voice! Sing, pray, and study Torah with your fellow worshippers.

Exalt, be happy, raise your voice, and join your prayer with those of your fellow Jews.

בְּשִׂמְחָה וּבְשָׂשׂוֹן הִנְחַלְתָּנוּ (41)

With joy and happiness You gave us a heritage.

A WOMAN OF WORTH

On these two facing pages you will learn to read some of the words found in the אֵשֶׁת חַיִל.

WORD ENDINGS

1 | יָד+■ֶיהָ=יָדֶיהָ |

בֵּן+■ֶיהָ=בָּנֶיהָ,   מַעֲשֶׂה+■ֶיהָ=מַעֲשֶׂיהָ.

2 | בַּעַל+■ָהּ=בַּעְלָהּ |

לְבוּשׁ+■ָהּ=לְבוּשָׁהּ,   בֵּית+■ָה=בֵּיתָהּ,

פָּתַח+■ָהּ=פָּתְחָה,   כַּף+■ָהּ=כַּפָּהּ,

לָשׁוֹן+■ָהּ=לְשׁוֹנָהּ,   יְהַלֵּל+■ָהּ=יְהַלְלָה

3 | בַּת+וֹת-בָּנוֹת |

רַב+וֹת=רַבּוֹת,   הֲלִיכָה+וֹת=הֲלִיכוֹת.

4 | שַׁעַר+■ִים=שְׁעָרִים |

פְּנִינָה+■ִים=פְּנִינִים.

WORD BEGINNINGS

1 הַ+חֵן=הַחֵן   הַ+יֹּפִי=הַיֹּפִי.

2 וְ+יְדֶיהָ=וְיָדֶיהָ   וְ+אַתְּ=וְאַתְּ,   וְ+לֹא=וְלֹא,   וְ+רָחוֹק=וְרָחוֹק,

וְ+הֶבֶל=וְהֶבֶל,   וְ+לֶחֶם=וְלֶחֶם,

וַ+יְהַלְלָהָ=וַיְהַלְלָהָ.   וְ+תוֹרַת=וְתוֹרַת,

WORD FAMILIES

1 בֵּן, בַּת, בָּנוֹת, בְּנָהּ.

2 אִשָּׁה, אֵשֶׁת.

TEFILLAH PHRASES

1 אֵשֶׁת חַיִל, בָּטַח בָּהּ, וְתוֹרַת חֶסֶד, גְּמָלַתְהוּ טוֹב.

2 רַבּוֹת בָּנוֹת, עַל לְשׁוֹנָהּ, תְּנוּ לָהּ, לֵב בַּעְלָהּ.

3 וְלֶחֶם עַצְלוּת, וִיהַלְלוּהָ בַשְּׁעָרִים, פִּיהָ פָּתְחָה.

4 נָטְעָה כָּרֶם, וְתוֹרַת-חֶסֶד, קָמוּ בָנֶיהָ.

5 יִרְאַת יְהוָֹה, כֹּל יְמֵי חַיֶּיהָ, כַּפָּהּ פָּרְשָׂה.

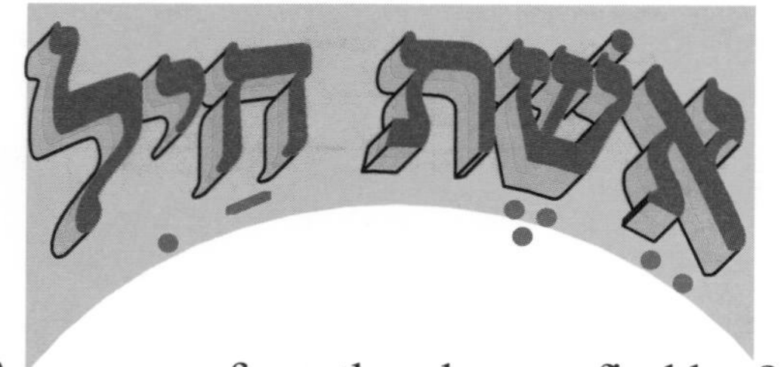

A WOMAN OF WORTH

The text for the poem אֵשֶׁת-חַיִל is from the Book of Proverbs 31:10–31.*

English	Hebrew
1. A woman of worth, who can find her?	אֵשֶׁת-חַיִל מִי יִמְצָא? 1
2. She is more precious than rubies	וְרָחוֹק מִפְּנִינִים מִכְרָהּ 2
3. Her husband trusts her	בָּטַח בָּהּ לֵב בַּעְלָהּ 3
4. And she will never lack gain.	וְשָׁלָל לֹא יֶחְסָר. 4
5. She does him only good	גְּמָלַתְהוּ טוֹב 5
6. And does not do evil all the days of her life.	וְלֹא רָע כֹּל יְמֵי חַיֶּיהָ. 6
7. She negotiates for a field and buys it.	זָמְמָה שָׂדֶה וַתִּקָּחֵהוּ. 7
8. With her own labor she plants a vineyard.	מִפְּרִי כַפֶּיהָ נָטְעָה כָּרֶם. 8
9. She reaches out to the poor	כַּפָּהּ פָּרְשָׂה לֶעָנִי 9
10. And helps those in need.	וְיָדֶיהָ שִׁלְּחָה לָאֶבְיוֹן. 10
11. She speaks with wisdom	פִּיהָ פָּתְחָה בְחָכְמָה 11
12. And the teaching of kIndness is on her tongue.	וְתוֹרַת חֶסֶד עַל לְשׁוֹנָהּ. 12
13. She looks at ways to enhance her home	צוֹפִיָּה הֲלִיכוֹת בֵּיתָה 13
14. And does not eat the bread of laziness.	וְלֶחֶם עַצְלוּת לֹא תֹאכֵל. 14
15. Her children rise and praise her,	קָמוּ בָנֶיהָ וַיְאַשְּׁרוּהָ 15
16. And her husband praises her.	בַּעְלָהּ וַיְהַלְלָהּ. 16
17. Many women acted with valor,	רַבּוֹת בָּנוֹת עָשׂוּ חָיִל 17
18. But you are the best of all.	וְאַתְּ עָלִית עַל כֻּלָּנָה. 18
19. Charm is false, and beauty fades,	שֶׁקֶר הַחֵן וְהֶבֶל הַיֹּפִי, 19
20. But a God-fearing woman is worthy of praise.	אִשָּׁה יִרְאַת יְהוָֹה הִיא תִתְהַלָּל. 20
21. Praise her for her good deeds,	תְּנוּ-לָהּ מִפְּרִי יָדֶיהָ, 21
22. Let her accomplishments be praised at the city gates.	וִיהַלְלוּהָ בַשְּׁעָרִים מַעֲשֶׂיהָ. 22

*Some verses have been omitted.

מִשְׁלֵי PROVERBS

מִשְׁלֵי (Proverbs) is one of the books in כְּתוּבִים, the third part of the תַּנַ"ךְ. The book of מִשְׁלֵי is a collection of wise sayings said to have been authored by King Solomon.

Your mother is a very special person with many skills. She is patient, creative, thoughtful, loving, gentle, funny, and smart.
Write her a note and say:

Dear Mom,
I love you very much. I love you because ________________________. I want you to know that despite my sometimes naughty behavior, I appreciate________________________. From now on I will try to listen and make the family ____________________________________.
Mom, I want you to know that you are super, and I'm glad you're you.
Mom, thousands of years ago our ancestors had mothers just like you. They called a woman like you an אֵשֶׁת חַיִל. I would like to read you several sentences from the אֵשֶׁת חַיִל poem.

Many of the ancient towns and cities were surrounded by stonewalls as fortifications to repel invaders and bands of raiders. The city walls were often massive stone structures with walkways on top to provide protection to the defenders. Square stone towers stood all along the wall. The city gates often had extra towers for defense.
The gate to the city was the busiest area. Much of the public life of the cities took place in or near the gates. There were markets with an array of stalls filled with vendors selling foods, spices, animals and handmade goods.
Frequently even the courts of law and parts of the city government were located near the city gates.

• • • • • • • • • • • • • • • • • • • •

In ancient days there were no stores that sold clothing or shoes or kitchen utensils. Almost everything had to be handmade. Grain was grown for bread, cattle were raised for meat and dairy products, flax and wool were woven into garments, and wood was shaped into tools, utensils, toys, and furniture.
The whole family—parents and children—worked from daylight to nightfall making themselves self-sufficient. Women were in charge of all phases of family endeavors. At home the אֵשֶׁת חַיִל was admired by her family. She was kind, gentle, dignified, and a source of family unity. In contrast to other societies at that time, the אֵשֶׁת חַיִל was also in some ways an independent woman. As the passages from אֵשֶׁת חַיִל show, she was involved in business and could purchase a piece of land and farm it.

HAVDALAH

On these two facing pages you will learn to read some of the words and phrases found in the ceremony of הַבְדָּלָה.

WORD ENDINGS

1 מִין+■ֵי=מִינֵי יָמִים+■ֵי=יְמֵי, מָאוֹר+■ֵי=מְאוֹרֵי.

2 בֹּשֶׂם+■ִים=בְּשָׂמִים עַם+■ִים=עַמִּים.

WORD BEGINNINGS

3 | הַ+גֶּפֶן=הַגָּפֶן |

הָ+עוֹלָם=הָעוֹלָם, הָ+אֵשׁ=הָאֵשׁ,

הַ+מַבְדִיל=הַמַּבְדִּיל, הַ+שְׁבִיעִי=הַשְּׁבִיעִי,

הַ+מַעֲשֶׂה=הַמַּעֲשֶׂה.

4 | לְ+חוֹל=לְחוֹל |

לְ+חֹשֶׁךְ=לְחֹשֶׁךְ, לְ+שֵׁשֶׁת=לְשֵׁשֶׁת.

WORD FAMILIES

1 יוֹם, יְמֵי.

2 אוֹר, מְאוֹרֵי.

TEFILLAH PHRASES

1 מִינֵי בְשָׂמִים, בֵּין יִשְׂרָאֵל, מֶלֶךְ הָעוֹלָם, פְּרִי הַגָּפֶן.

2 מְאוֹרֵי הָאֵשׁ, קֹדֶשׁ לְחוֹל, בֵּין אוֹר לְחֹשֶׁךְ, יְמֵי הַמַּעֲשֶׂה.

3 יוֹם הַשְּׁבִיעִי, יִשְׂרָאֵל לָעַמִּים, בָּרוּךְ אַתָּה יְיָ.

HAVDALAH

The Kiddush marks the Shabbat as a day of rest. The הַבְדָּלָה marks the end of Shabbat and the beginning of a week of work.

The blessing over the wine

1. Blessed is Adonai	1 בָּרוּךְ אַתָּה יְיָ
2. Our God, Ruler of the universe,	2 אֱלֹהֵינוּ מֶלֶךְ הָעוֹלָם,
3. Who created the fruit of the vine.	3 בּוֹרֵא פְּרִי הַגָּפֶן.

The blessing over the spices:

4. Blessed is Adonai	4 בָּרוּךְ אַתָּה יְיָ
5. Our God, Ruler of the universe,	5 אֱלֹהֵינוּ מֶלֶךְ הָעוֹלָם,
6. Creator of a variety of spices	6 בּוֹרֵא מִינֵי בְשָׂמִים.

The blessing over the havdalah candle:

7. Blessed is Adonai	7 בָּרוּךְ אַתָּה יְיָ
8. Our God, Ruler of the universe,	8 אֱלֹהֵינוּ מֶלֶךְ הָעוֹלָם,
9. Creator of the lights of fire	9 בּוֹרֵא מְאוֹרֵי הָאֵשׁ.

10. Blessed are you, Adonai	10 בָּרוּךְ אַתָּה יְיָ
11. Our God, Ruler of the universe,	11 אֱלֹהֵינוּ מֶלֶךְ הָעוֹלָם,
12. Who has made distinction between holy and ordinary,	12 הַמַּבְדִּיל בֵּין קֹדֶשׁ לְחוֹל,
13. Between light and darkness,	13 בֵּין אוֹר לְחֹשֶׁךְ,
14. Between Israel and other nations,	14 בֵּין יִשְׂרָאֵל לָעַמִּים,
15. Between the seventh day	15 בֵּין יוֹם הַשְּׁבִיעִי
16 And the six work days.	16 לְשֵׁשֶׁת יְמֵי הַמַּעֲשֶׂה.
17. Blessed are you, Adonai,	17 בָּרוּךְ אַתָּה יהוה,
18. Who has made distinction between holy and ordinary.	18 הַמַּבְדִּיל בֵּין קֹדֶשׁ לְחוֹל.

HAVDALAH הַבְדָלָה

The Havdalah ceremony takes place when three stars can be seen in the Saturday night sky. For the הַבְדָלָה ceremony you will need three things:
1. A cup of wine. 2. A braided הַבְדָלָה candle. 3. בְּשָׂמִים (sweet-smelling spices).

HOW TO PERFORM THE הַבְדָלָה CEREMONY

1. A Kiddush cup is filled with wine, the blessing is recited and the wine is sipped.
2. Raise the בְּשָׂמִים box, recite the blessing and pass the spice box so everyone can enjoy the aroma.
3. Recite the third blessing over the lighted הַבְדָלָה candle. Participants can look at the reflections of the flame on their fingernails.
4. The final prayer, הַמַּבְדִּיל, is recited.
5. Some families end the service by singing אֵלִיָּהוּ הַנָּבִיא ("Elijah the Prophet").
6. The הַבְדָלָה light is put out and Shabbat is officially over.
7. Everyone wishes each other a שָׁבוּעַ טוֹב ("good, week").

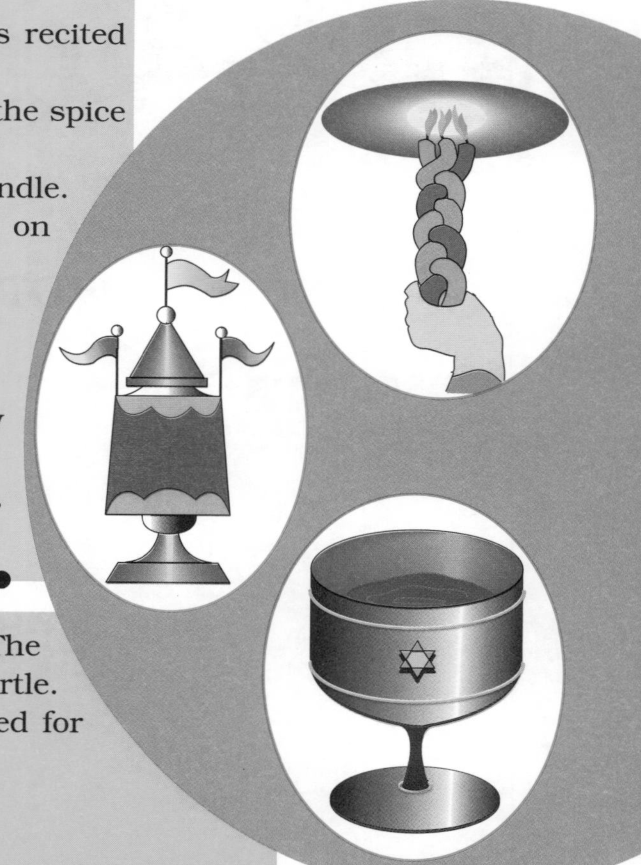

The holder containing the spices is called a הֲדַס. The name comes from the word הֲדַס which means myrtle. In olden days only the myrtle (הֲדַס) spice was used for the הַבְדָלָה ceremony.

God's miracles touch you in many ways. With your nose you can smell the scent of beautiful flowers and the scent of freshly baked cookies and hallah. With your ears you can hear the music of a rushing stream. With your hands you can feel the cold of the snow and with your tongue taste the sweetness of honey and juice of freshly squeezed oranges. With your eyes you can see the colors of the rainbow and your reflection in a mirror. God's miraculous creations awaken all the senses of your body and your mind.

As you participate in the הַבְדָלָה ceremony, taste the wine, smell the spices, see the flame and touch the candle. Think of the miracle of your senses and say a silent prayer for the blessings God has given you.

THE TEN COMMANDMENTS

On these two facing pages you will learn to read some of the words and phrases found in the עֲשֶׂרֶת הַדִּבְּרוֹת.

WORD ENDINGS

1 דָּבָר+■ִים=דְּבָרִים   עֶבֶד+■ִים=עֲבָדִים,   אַחֵר+■ִים=אֲחֵרִים,

יוֹם+■ִים=יָמִים .

2 אֱלֹהִים+■ֶיךָ=אֱלֹהֶיךָ   יָמִים+■ֶיךָ=יָמֶיךָ .

1 הוֹצֵאתִי+ךָ=הוֹצֵאתִיךָ   מְלָאכָה+ךָ=מְלַאכְתֶּךָ,   אֵם+ךָ=אִמֶּךָ,

רֵעֶה+ךָ=רֵעֶךָ .

WORD BEGINNINGS

1 הַ+דְבָרִים=הַדְּבָרִים הַ+אֵלֶּה=הָאֵלֶּה, הַ+שַׁבָּת=הַשַּׁבָּת,

הַ+שְׁבִיעִי=הַשְּׁבִיעִי, הַ+אֲדָמָה=הָאֲדָמָה.

2 תִּ+רָצַח=תִּרְצָח תִּ+נָאַף=תִּנְאָף, תִּ+גָנַב=תִּגְנֹב,

תִּ+נָשָׂא=תִּשָּׂא.

3 וְ+יוֹם=וְיוֹם וְ+עָשִׂיתָ=וְעָשִׂיתָ, וְ+אֵת=וְאֵת.

WORD FAMILIES

1 אֱלֹהִים, אֱלֹהֶיךָ. רֵעֶךָ, בְּרֵעֲךָ. וַיְדַבֵּר, הַדְּבָרִים.

2 לְךָ, לָךְ. עֲבָדִים, תַּעֲבֹד.

TEFILLAH PHRASES

1 אֵת כָּל הַדְּבָרִים, בֵּית רֵעֶךָ, לֹא תִּנְאָף, לֹא תַחְמֹד.

2 מֵאֶרֶץ מִצְרַיִם, אָנֹכִי יְיָ אֱלֹהֶיךָ, אֱלֹהִים אֲחֵרִים.

3 זָכוֹר אֶת-יוֹם הַשַּׁבָּת, שֵׁשֶׁת יָמִים תַּעֲבֹד, לַייָ אֱלֹהֶיךָ.

4 לֹא-תַעֲנֶה בְרֵעֲךָ, אֲשֶׁר הוֹצֵאתִיךָ, כַּבֵּד אֶת-אָבִיךָ.

5 עַל הָאֲדָמָה, לֹא תִּרְצָח, לְמַעַן יַאֲרִכוּן יָמֶיךָ.

THE TEN COMMANDMENTS

On Shavuot the Torah portion containing the עֲשֶׂרֶת הַדִּבְּרוֹת is read. In some synagogues it is customary for the congregants to stand and to repeat the עֲשֶׂרֶת הַדִּבְּרוֹת with the Torah reader.

English	Commandment	Hebrew
1. And God spoke		וַיְדַבֵּר אֱלֹהִים 1
2. All of these words, saying:		אֵת כָּל הַדְּבָרִים הָאֵלֶּה לֵאמֹר: 2
3. I am Adonai your God,	***1***	אָנֹכִי יהוה אֱלֹהֶיךָ, 3
4. Who brought you out of the land of Egypt,		אֲשֶׁר הוֹצֵאתִיךָ מֵאֶרֶץ מִצְרַיִם, 4
5. From the house of slavery.		מִבֵּית עֲבָדִים. 5
6. You shall have no other gods besides Me	***2***	לֹא יִהְיֶה לְךָ אֱלֹהִים אֲחֵרִים עַל-פָּנָי 6
7. You shall not take the name of Adonai in vain.	***3***	לֹא תִשָּׂא אֶת שֵׁם יהוה אֱלֹהֶיךָ לַשָּׁוְא. 7
8. Remember the Shabbat and keep it holy.	***4***	זָכוֹר אֶת יוֹם הַשַּׁבָּת לְקַדְּשׁוֹ. 8
9. You shall work six days,		שֵׁשֶׁת יָמִים תַּעֲבֹד, 9
10. And you will do all your work,		וְעָשִׂיתָ כָּל מְלַאכְתֶּךָ, 10
11. And the seventh day is the Shabbat		וְיוֹם הַשְּׁבִיעִי שַׁבָּת 11
12. For Adonai your God.		לַיהוה אֱלֹהֶיךָ. 12
13. Honor your father and your mother,	***5***	כַּבֵּד אֶת-אָבִיךָ וְאֶת-אִמֶּךָ, 13
14. So that your days on earth will be lengthened,		לְמַעַן יַאֲרִכוּן יָמֶיךָ עַל הָאֲדָמָה, 14
15. which the Lord gives you.		אֲשֶׁר יהוה אֱלֹהֶיךָ נֹתֵן לָךְ. 15
16. You shall not murder.	***6***	לֹא תִרְצָח. 16
17. You shall not be unfaithful.	***7***	לֹא תִנְאָף. 17
18. You shall not steal.	***8***	לֹא תִגְנֹב. 18
19. You shall not be a false witness.	***9***	לֹא-תַעֲנֶה בְרֵעֲךָ עֵד שָׁקֶר. 19
20. You shall not desire the house of your neighbor.	***10***	לֹא תַחְמֹד בֵּית רֵעֶךָ. 20

The Commandments are a ten-channel, astral radio receiver, tuned into God. When you feel uneasy and sense that something is just not right, turn on your receiver and tune into the TC channel.

If someone asks to take something that does not belong to you tune in to channel 8. If someone asks you to spread gossip, try tuning into channel 9.

When you do this, you will hear a loud, clear voice telling you the right thing to do. The Ten Commandments inner voice is our guide to the Jewish way of life.

The Ten Commandments were given to the Israelites twice. The first time, Moses smashed the tablets because he found the Israelites worshiping a Golden Calf.

God then told Moses to climb Mount Sinai again to receive two more tablets of stone. Moses stayed on the mountain top for forty days and forty nights. This time, when Moses came down, the Children of Israel were waiting for him. They bowed their heads and promised to obey the Commandments.

In the Ten Commandments, the cornerstone of the Jewish faith, only one holiday is mentioned— שַׁבָּת. The Fourth Commandment says in part, "Remember the שַׁבָּת day and keep it holy. Six days shall you labor and do all your work. But the seventh day is the שַׁבָּת of Adonai, your God." This commandment gave something to the world that it never had before — a weekly day of rest.

THE HOPE

***On these two facing pages you will learn to read some of the words and phrases found in the* הַתִּקְוָה.**

WORD ENDINGS

פָּנִים+■ָה=פְּנִימָה 1   קָדִים+■ָה=קָדִימָה.

תִּקְוָה+נוּ=תִּקְוָתֵנוּ 2   אֶרֶץ+נוּ=אַרְצֵנוּ.

יָהוּד+■ִי=יְהוּדִי 3   חֹפֶשׁ+■ִי=חָפְשִׁי.

WORD BEGINNINGS

1 בְּ+אֶרֶץ=בְּאֶרֶץ   בְּ+אַרְצֵנוּ=בְּאַרְצֵנוּ

WORD FAMILIES

1 הַתִּקְוָה, תִּקְוָתֵנוּ, בְּאֶרֶץ, בְּאַרְצֵנוּ.

TEFILLAH PHRASES

1 בְּאֶרֶץ צִיּוֹן, עַם חָפְשִׁי, נֶפֶשׁ יְהוּדִי, עַיִן לְצִיּוֹן.

2 עוֹד לֹא, שְׁנוֹת אַלְפַּיִם, וּלְפַאֲתֵי מִזְרָח.

THE HOPE

הַתִּקְוָה ("The Hope"), the Jewish national anthem, was written in 1878 by Naphtali Herz Imber. הַתִּקְוָה is about hope, the undying two-thousand-year hope of the Jewish people to return to their homeland, Israel.

1. As long as in the heart,	1 כָּל עוֹד בַּלֵּבָב פְּנִימָה
2. A Jewish spirit sings,	2 נֶפֶשׁ יְהוּדִי הוֹמִיָּה
3. And towards the East,	3 וּלְפַאֲתֵי מִזְרָח קָדִימָה
4. The eyes look toward Zion.	4 עַיִן לְצִיּוֹן צוֹפִיָּה.
5. Our hope is still not lost,	5 עוֹד לֹא אָבְדָה תִקְוָתֵנוּ
6. Our hope of 2,000 years,	6 הַתִּקְוָה שְׁנוֹת אַלְפַּיִם
7. To be a free nation in our own land,	7 לִהְיוֹת עַם חָפְשִׁי בְּאַרְצֵנוּ
8. In the land of Zion and Jerusalem.	8 בְּאֶרֶץ צִיּוֹן וִירוּשָׁלָיִם.

When you sing the Hatikvah, you are doing much more than just singing a nice melody. You are making a promise. You are promising that you will never forget that undying Jewish hope for independence. You are promising that you will do all within your power to help the State of Israel prosper.

You can help. You can buy products made in Israel, and you can plant trees in Israel by contributing to the Jewish National Fund. You can support Israel Bond drives. You can study the Hebrew language, and you can spend time in Israel as campers, students, tourists, and maybe someday as olim—new immigrants to the Jewish homeland

You can also help by learning about Israel and the Israelis and by studying Jewish history. The more you understand the Jewish homeland, the more you will learn to love and value Israel, and the more you will be able to do to help the survival and the growth of Israel.

צִיּוֹן

צִיּוֹן is another name for Israel and Jerusalem. In the synagogue, the Holy Ark where the Torah is kept, always faces in the direction of צִיּוֹן. As we pray along with the congregation, our eyes, our hearts, and our prayers are directed toward Israel and Jerusalem.

יְרוּשָׁלַיִם

High in the Judean mountains in the heart of Israel stands the ancient and modern capital of Israel, יְרוּשָׁלַיִם. Some people say the name Jerusalem is made up of two words: יְרוּ, meaning "city of," and שָׁלַיִם, meaning "peace." Wherever Jews were scattered during the two thousand years of exile, they prayed for the return to צִיּוֹן, the biblical name for יְרוּשָׁלַיִם. Every Passover, at the end of the seder, Jews sing the hopeful לְשָׁנָה הַבָּאָה בִּירוּשָׁלָיִם prayer, "Next year in Jerusalem." When King David unified Israel in the tenth century B.C.E., he made יְרוּשָׁלַיִם the capital of his kingdom. King Solomon, David's son, built the glorious Temple there. In 70 C.E. the Romans destroyed יְרוּשָׁלַיִם and for two thousand years it was ruled by conquerors. In 1948, after two thousand years of exile, the modern city of יְרוּשָׁלַיִם once more became the capital of the rebuilt State of Israel.

שִׁיבַת צִיּוֹן

Wherever Jews lived during their two thousand years of exile, they recited special prayers for the return to Zion. These prayers are called שִׁיבַת צִיּוֹן prayers. Zion is another name for Israel and Jerusalem. As we pray we face east toward Israel. The prayers direct our hearts and minds toward the miracle of the Jewish homeland. The first stanza of the הַתִּקְוָה directs our hearts and spirits toward Zion.

הַתִּקְוָה

In 70 C.E., the Roman General Titus destroyed the city of יְרוּשָׁלַיִם and exiled all its inhabitants. For two thousand years, Jews never lost hope that someday they would return. In 1948, the hope became a reality.

סֵמֶל

The סֵמֶל (emblem) of the modern State of Israel consists of the ancient seven-branched Temple menorah. The menorah is surrounded by two olive branches. The olive trees provided the oil for the golden menorah in the Holy Temple. Olive branches are also an ancient סֵמֶל of peace and harmony.

JEWISH NATIONAL FUND

The Return to Zion was sponsored by the Jewish National Fund. The land for the settlements in Israel was purchased by the Jewish National Fund, which was established in 1901. The Jewish National Fund depended upon small sums of money collected throughout the world. The little blue-and-white Jewish Nation-al Fund box found a place in millions of Jewish homes all over the world.

דֶּגֶל

The blue-and-white Israeli flag was designed in 1897 by David Wolffsohn at the first Zionist Congress. According to Wolffsohn blue and white were chosen because they were the colors of the טַלִּית which Jews wear when they pray. The מָגֵן דָּוִד (Star of David) was chosen because legend tells us that King David decorated his shield with a מָגֵן דָּוִד.

LIGHTING THE HANUKAH CANDLES

On these two facing pages you will learn to read some of the words found in הַדְלָקַת נֵרוֹת שֶׁל חֲנֻכָּה.

WORD ENDINGS

1 קִדֵּשׁ+נוּ=קִדְּשָׁנוּ

וְקִיֵּם+נוּ=וְקִיְּמָנוּ, הֶחֱיָה+נוּ=הֶחֱיָנוּ,
וְהִגִּיעַ+נוּ=וְהִגִּיעָנוּ.

2 נֵס+ִים=נִסִּים

יוֹם+ִים=יָמִים, קָדוֹשׁ+ִים=קְדוֹשִׁים.

3 נֵר+וֹת=נֵרוֹת

נִפְלָא+וֹת=נִפְלָאוֹת, תְּשׁוּעָה+וֹת=תְּשׁוּעוֹת,
מִלְחָמָה+וֹת=מִלְחָמוֹת.

4 שֵׁם+ךָ=שִׁמְךָ

יְשׁוּעָה+ךָ=יְשׁוּעָתֶךָ, נִפְלָאוֹת+ךָ=נִפְלְאוֹתֶיךָ,
כֹּהֲנִים+ךָ=כֹּהֲנֶיךָ.

WORD BEGINNINGS

1 הָ+עוֹלָם=הָעוֹלָם

הָ+הֵם=הָהֵם, הַ+נֵּרוֹת=הַנֵּרוֹת,
הַ+נִפְלָאוֹת=הַנִּפְלָאוֹת,
הַ+תְּשׁוּעוֹת=הַתְּשׁוּעוֹת,
הַ+מִלְחָמוֹת=הַמִּלְחָמוֹת,
הַ+קְדוֹשִׁים=הַקְּדוֹשִׁים.

2 בַּ+זְמַן=בַּזְּמַן

בַּ+יָמִים= בַּיָּמִים.

3 וְ+צִוָּנוּ=וְצִוָּנוּ

וְ+קִיְּמָנוּ=וְקִיְּמָנוּ, וְ+הִגִּיעָנוּ=וְהִגִּיעָנוּ,
וְ+עַל=וְעַל, וְ+כָל=וְכָל, וְ+אֵין=וְאֵין.

4 לְ+הַדְלִיק=לְהַדְלִיק

לְ+הוֹדוֹת=לְהוֹדוֹת, לְ+הַלֵּל=לְ+הַלֵּל,
לְ+הִשְׁתַּמֵּשׁ=לְהִשְׁתַּמֵּשׁ, לְ+שִׁמְךָ=לְשִׁמְךָ,
לַ+אֲבוֹתֵינוּ=לַאֲבוֹתֵינוּ, לַ+זְמַן=לַזְּמַן.

5 שֶׁ+עָשָׂה=שֶׁעָשָׂה

שֶׁ+עָשִׂיתָ=שֶׁעָשִׂיתָ.

TEFILLAH PHRASES

1 לְהַדְלִיק נֵר, שֶׁהֶחֱיָנוּ וְקִיְּמָנוּ, הַנֵּרוֹת הַלָּלוּ, עַל יְדֵי כֹּהֲנֶךָ.
2 קִדְּשָׁנוּ בְּמִצְוֹתָיו, וְעַל יְשׁוּעָתֶךָ, אֲנַחְנוּ מַדְלִיקִין, וְאֵין לָנוּ רְשׁוּת.
3 שֶׁעָשִׂיתָ לַאֲבוֹתֵינוּ, וּלְהַלֵּל לְשִׁמְךָ הַגָּדוֹל, שְׁמוֹנַת יְמֵי חֲנֻכָּה.
4 בַּיָּמִים הָהֵם, כְּדֵי לְהוֹדוֹת, שֶׁעָשָׂה נִסִּים לַאֲבוֹתֵינוּ.

HANUKAH BLESSINGS

The holiday of Hanukah begins on the 25th of Kislev. The rededication of the Temple took place in 165 B.C.E.

Before lighting the hanukiah say:

1. Blessed are you, Adonai	1 בָּרוּךְ אַתָּה יהוה,
2. Our God, Ruler of the universe,	2 אֱלֹהֵינוּ מֶלֶךְ הָעוֹלָם,
3. Who has made us holy with Mitzvot	3 אֲשֶׁר קִדְּשָׁנוּ בְּמִצְוֹתָיו*,
4. And commanded us to light the Hanukah candles.	4 וְצִוָּנוּ לְהַדְלִיק נֵר שֶׁל חֲנֻכָּה.
5. Blessed are you, Adonai	5 בָּרוּךְ אַתָּה יהוה,
6. Our God, Ruler of the universe,	6 אֱלֹהֵינוּ מֶלֶךְ הָעוֹלָם,
7. Who performed miracles for our ancestors	7 שֶׁעָשָׂה נִסִּים לַאֲבוֹתֵינוּ,
8. In those days at this time of year.	8 בַּיָּמִים הָהֵם בַּזְּמַן הַזֶּה.

This blessing is recited only on the first night:

9. Blessed are you, Adonai	9 בָּרוּךְ אַתָּה יהוה
10. Our God, Ruler of the universe,	10 אֱלֹהֵינוּ מֶלֶךְ הָעוֹלָם,
11. Who has kept us alive and helped us	11 שֶׁהֶחֱיָנוּ וְקִיְּמָנוּ
12. And brought us to this season.	12 וְהִגִּיעָנוּ לַזְּמַן הַזֶּה.

After lighting the hanukiah say:

13. These candles that we light today	13 הַנֵּרוֹת הַלָּלוּ אֲנַחְנוּ מַדְלִיקִין,
14. Are for the miracles and wonders,	14 עַל הַנִּסִּים וְעַל הַנִּפְלָאוֹת,
15. The victories and the battles,	15 וְעַל הַתְּשׁוּעוֹת וְעַל הַמִּלְחָמוֹת,
16. Which You performed for our ancestors,	16 שֶׁעָשִׂיתָ לַאֲבוֹתֵינוּ,
17. In those days, at this time of year.	17 בַּיָּמִים הָהֵם בַּזְּמַן הַזֶּה,
18. Through the deeds of Your priests (the Maccabees)	18 עַל יְדֵי כֹּהֲנֶךָ הַקְּדוֹשִׁים.

19. All eight days of Hanukah	19 וְכָל שְׁמוֹנַת יְמֵי חֲנֻכָּה,
20. These candles are holy and	20 הַנֵּרוֹת הַלָּלוּ קֹדֶשׁ הֵם,
21. And we are not permitted to use them	21 וְאֵין לָנוּ רְשׁוּת לְהִשְׁתַּמֵּשׁ בָּהֶם,
22. But only to look at them.	22 אֶלָּא לִראוֹתָם בִּלְבָד.
21. Just to thank and praise Your mighty name	21 כְּדֵי לְהוֹדוֹת וּלְהַלֵּל לְשִׁמְךָ הַגָּדוֹל,
22. For Your miracles, Your deliverance,	22 עַל נִסֶּיךָ וְעַל יְשׁוּעָתֶךָ,
23. And Your wonders.	23 וְעַל נִפְלְאוֹתֶיךָ.

HOW DID THE HOLIDAY OF חֲנֻכָּה GET ITS NAME?

The Hebrew word Hanukah means "dedication". After the Maccabees recaptured Jerusalem, they cleaned the Holy Temple and dedicated it once more. The miracle of the holy oil took place at the dedication.

HOW TO LIGHT THE חֲנֻכָּה CANDLES

1) The חֲנֻכִּיָּה has places for eight candles. There is also a place for one special candle in front or on top of all the others. This special candle, with which we light all the other candles, is called the שַׁמָּשׁ.
2) On the first night of חֲנֻכָּה, you face the חֲנֻכִּיָּה and put one candle into the holder at your extreme right.
3) You hold the lighted שַׁמָּשׁ in one hand, and begin chanting the first blessing.
4) After chanting the first blessing, you light the candle at the extreme right.
5) Then say the second blessing and the שֶׁהֶחֱיָנוּ prayer.
The שֶׁהֶחֱיָנוּ is said only on the first night of Hanukah. After singing the blessings you sing the hymn Maoz Tzur.

On חֲנֻכָּה it is traditional to serve potato latkes, cheese dishes and sufganiot (jelly doughnuts). What is the reason for serving latkes? Some say that we serve potato latkes fried in oil in memory of the miraculous jar of holy oil which burned for eight days. The ancient temple menorah was lit with olive oil. Some people continue the same tradition and use olive oil instead of candles. Judith. also associated with Hanukah, served Holofernes cheese dishes before cutting off his head

On חֲנֻכָּה Jews all over the world remind themselves and all the world of what freedom is and of God's role in the Maccabean victory. Brightly burning candles, happy songs, spinning draydels, and crunchy latkes remind us of the ideals and joys of Hanukah.
On חֲנֻכָּה you thank God for "the miracles and wonders that God has performed for our ancestors."

Today we know more about the חֲנֻכָּה story because of the Books of Maccabees. First and Second Maccabees belong to a group of post-biblical writings known as the Apocrypha. The original version of this book, written in Hebrew, was lost. Fortunately, the Hebrew text had been translated into Greek. It was preserved in the Septaugint, the Greek version of the Bible. Although the authors of Maccabees are unknown, several facts about them are known. They were Jews, who lived sometime after the Maccabean revolt. From their first-hand knowledge, it is believed that they were familiar with the events of the uprising. The text starts with a summary history of the conquest of Alexander the Great, and the origin of the Seleucid Empire. It retells historical events from Antiochus IV (175 B.C.E.) to the death of Simon the Hasmonean in 135 B.C.E.

HOW WAS THE ORIGINAL TEMPLE MENORAH CONSTRUCTED?

The Torah (Exodus 25:31-40) provides the construction details of the Temple menorah. It was made by Bezalel and hammered out of a solid slab of gold. According to the Torah, it stood seven feet tall, weighed 100 pounds, and was seven-branched.

According to some commentators, the seven-branched מְנוֹרָה, represents the creation of the world in six days, and the center light is for the seventh day—the Sabbath.

Our sages say that the original Mosaic menorah was concealed by the priests prior to the destruction of the First Temple and has never been found.

The מְנוֹרָה of the Second Temple was made to resemble the one in the Tabernacle, as shown on the relief on the Arch of Titus. It shows the מְנוֹרָה is carried on poles on the shoulders of Roman soldiers in a triumphal procession through the streets of Rome.

WHAT IS THE DIFFERENCE BETWEEN A מְנוֹרָה AND A חֲנֻכִּיָּה ?

There are two different candelabras used in Jewish religious ceremonies. A מְנוֹרָה is a seven-branched candelabra. According to the Torah (Exodus 37:17) the first מְנוֹרָה was made of gold by the artist Bezalel for the portable desert Tabernacle.

When the Maccabees recaptured Jerusalem they cleaned and rededicated the Temple. They rekindled a wooden replica of the seven-branched Temple מְנוֹרָה. The golden מְנוֹרָה had been stolen by the Seleucids.

A חֲנֻכִּיָּה is a nine-branched candelabra which is used on the holiday of Hanukah. Eight branches are for the eight days of Hanukah. The ninth branch is called the shamash. שַׁמָּשׁ is a Hebrew word meaning "helper." The שַׁמָּשׁ is used to light the other candles in the חֲנֻכִּיָּה.

THE FOUR QUESTIONS

On these two facing pages you will learn to read some of the words found in the
אַרְבַּע קֻשְׁיוֹת.

WORD ENDINGS

1 | לַיְלָה+וֹת=לֵילוֹת | יָרָק+וֹת=יְרָקוֹת, מַצָּה+וֹת=מַצּוֹת .

2 | אוֹכֵל+■ִין=אוֹכְלִין | מֵסֵב+■ִין=מְסֻבִּין, מַטְבִּיל+■ִין=מַטְבִּילִין,
יוֹשֵׁב+■ִין=יוֹשְׁבִין.

3 | אֱלֹהִים+ֵנוּ=אֱלֹהֵינוּ | צִוָּה+נוּ=צִוָּנוּ .

WORD BEGINNINGS

1 הַ+לַיְלָה=הַלַּיְלָה הַ+זֶה=הַזֶּה, הַ+לֵילוֹת=הַלֵּילוֹת,

הָ+עוֹלָם=הָעוֹלָם .

2 וּ+בֵין=וּבֵין וּ+מַצָּה=וּמַצָּה .

3 בְּ+כָל=בְּכָל בְּ+מִצְוֹתָיו=בְּמִצְוֹתָיו.

WORD FAMILIES

1 כָּל, בְּכָל, כֻּלָּנוּ. כֻּלּוֹ. לַיְלָה, לֵילוֹת.

2 אוֹכֵל, אֲכִילַת, אוֹכְלִין. פַּעַם, פְּעָמִים.

TEFILLAH PHRASES

1 אֲכִילַת מָרוֹר, מֶלֶךְ הָעוֹלָם, קִדְּשָׁנוּ בְּמִצְוֹתָיו, אֲכִילַת מַצָּה.

2 מַה נִּשְׁתַּנָּה, חָמֵץ וּמַצָּה, כֻּלָּנוּ מְסֻבִּין, שְׁתֵּי פְעָמִים.

3 אָנוּ אוֹכְלִין, מִכָּל הַלֵּילוֹת, שְׁאָר יְרָקוֹת, פַּעַם אֶחָת, כֻּלּוֹ מַצָּה.

4 שֶׁבְּכָל הַלֵּילוֹת, אֵין אָנוּ מַטְבִּילִין, , הַלַּיְלָה הַזֶּה.

THE FOUR QUESTIONS

***The Seder ceremony is a time for Torah study and discussion. The learning session starts with the youngest child asking the four questions–* אַרְבַּע קֻשְׁיוֹת.**

1. Why is this night different	מַה נִּשְׁתַּנָּה הַלַּיְלָה הַזֶּה, 1
2. From all other nights?	מִכָּל הַלֵּילוֹת? 2
	1
3. On all other nights	שֶׁבְּכָל הַלֵּילוֹת, 3
4. We eat leavened or unleavened bread (matzah);	אָנוּ אוֹכְלִין חָמֵץ וּמַצָּה. 4
5. On this night why only unleavened bread (matzah)?	הַלַּיְלָה הַזֶּה כֻּלּוֹ מַצָּה. 5
	2
6. On all other nights	שֶׁבְּכָל הַלֵּילוֹת, 6
7. We eat all kinds of herbs;	אָנוּ אוֹכְלִין שְׁאָר יְרָקוֹת, 7
8. On this night why only bitter herbs?	הַלַּיְלָה הַזֶּה מָרוֹר. 8
	3
9. On all other nights	שֶׁבְּכָל הַלֵּילוֹת 9
10. We do not dip our herbs even once;	אֵין אָנוּ מַטְבִּילִין אֲפִילוּ פַּעַם אֶחָת. 10
11. On this night why do we dip twice?	הַלַּיְלָה הַזֶּה שְׁתֵּי פְעָמִים. 11
	4
12. On all other nights	שֶׁבְּכָל הַלֵּילוֹת, 12
13. We eat either sitting or reclining;	אָנוּ אוֹכְלִין בֵּין יוֹשְׁבִין וּבֵין מְסֻבִּין. 13
14. On this night why do we only recline?	הַלַּיְלָה הַזֶּה כֻּלָּנוּ מְסֻבִּין. 14

Blessing over the matzah:

15. Blessed are you, Adonai	15 בָּרוּךְ אַתָּה יהוה,
16. Our God, Ruler of the universe,	16 אֱלֹהֵינוּ מֶלֶךְ הָעוֹלָם,
17. Who made us holy with Mitzvot	17 אֲשֶׁר קִדְּשָׁנוּ בְּמִצְוֹתָיו,
18. And commanded us to eat matzah.	18 וְצִוָּנוּ עַל אֲכִילַת מַצָּה:

Blessing over the bitter herbs:

19. Blessed are you, Adonai	19 בָּרוּךְ אַתָּה יהוה,
20. Our God, Ruler of the universe	20 אֱלֹהֵינוּ מֶלֶךְ הָעוֹלָם,
21. Who has made us holy with Mitzvot	21 אֲשֶׁר קִדְּשָׁנוּ בְּמִצְוֹתָיו,
22. And commanded us to eat bitter herbs.	22 וְצִוָּנוּ עַל אֲכִילַת מָרוֹר:

POOR PERSON'S BREAD לַחְמָא עַנְיָא

Matzah is called לַחְמָא עַנְיָא because, like poor person's bread, it is made only with flour, without nourishing ingredients like eggs and milk. And, like poor person's bread it is hard to eat and digest.

NEXT YEAR IN JERUSALEM

We end the Seder with the Hebrew לְשָׁנָה הַבָּאָה בִּירוּשָׁלָיִם Next year in Jerusalem.

Our people began in the land of Israel thousands of years ago. Our people loved the land of Israel. They used to say that Israel was the center of the world. And right in the middle of Israel was Jerusalem and the Holy Temple.

Why do we recite לַחְמָא עַנְיָא at the Seder? Because Passover is also known as the Festival of Freedom. On Passover we celebrate the freeing of the slaves from Egypt. When we recite this prayer we also remind ourselves that there are still many people who are poor and need help.

Today, a special fund for the poor מָעוֹת חִטִּים ("money for wheat") is collected and distributed before Passover. It is a mitzvah to share with others. Helping and sharing is something God wants us to do. When we share we are making the world a better place in which to live.

יְרוּשָׁלַיִם

Why do we Jews love Israel and Jerusalem? Because the greatest things that ever happened in Jewish history took place in Jerusalem. King Solomon built the Holy Temple in Jerusalem. Great Jewish kings ruled in Jerusalem. Many miracles happened in Jerusalem. Three times a year, on Sukkot, Pesach and Shavout, Jewish farmers brought sacrifices to the Holy Temple in Jerusalem. So holy is Jerusalem that we recite our prayers facing Jerusalem to our east.

זְמַן חֵרוּתֵינוּ

Passover is also called זְמַן חֵרוּתֵינוּ, the season of our freedom. On Passover the Israelites were freed from slavery in Egypt. Jews believe that every person in the world should be free. No person should have to serve another against their will.

On the Liberty Bell, in Philadelphia, the words of the Bible are inscribed: "Proclaim liberty throughout the land for all its inhabitants (Leviticus 25:10).

I BELIEVE אֲנִי מַאֲמִין

In some homes a new ceremony has been introduced before opening the door for Elijah the Prophet. During the ceremony we remember the six-million Jews who were murdered by the Nazis and the heroes of the ghetto revolts.
We sing the song אֲנִי מַאֲמִין. This Song of Hope was sung by the martyrs in the concentration camps.
The words were written in accordance with the teachings of the famous Jewish philosopher, Moses Maimonides.

אֲנִי מַאֲמִין I believe
אֲנִי מַאֲמִין. I believe
אֲנִי מַאֲמִין I believe.
בֶּאֱמוּנָה שְׁלֵמָה With all my faith
בֶּאֱמוּנָה שְׁלֵמָה. With all my faith.
בְּבִיאַת הַמָּשִׁיחַ That the Messiah will come
בְּבִיאַת הַמָּשִׁיחַ That the Messiah will come.
אֲנִי מַאֲמִין I believe . . .

PRIESTS כֹּהֲנִים

All Priests and Levites, are descendants of the tribe of Levi. Aaron and his descendants were given the honor of the priesthood, because he was the brother of Moses. He helped free the Israelites from Egyptian slavery.

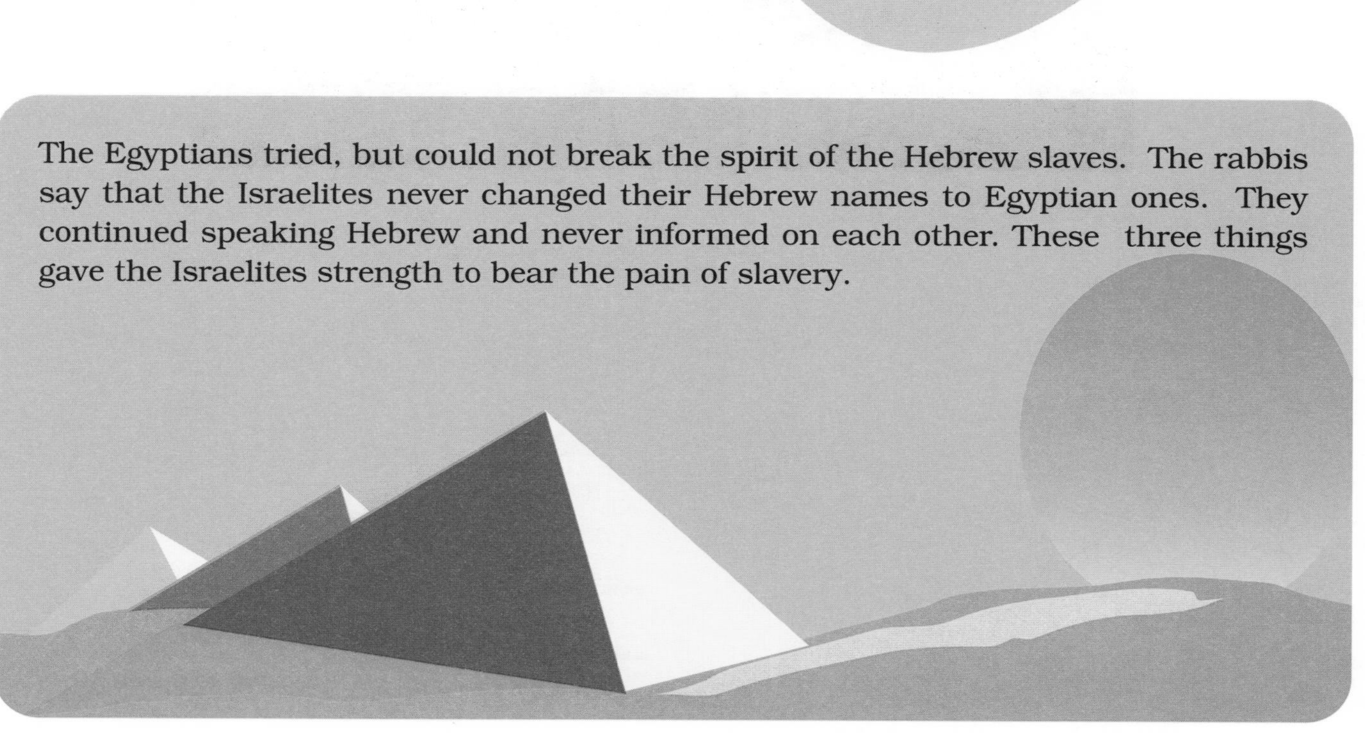

The Egyptians tried, but could not break the spirit of the Hebrew slaves. The rabbis say that the Israelites never changed their Hebrew names to Egyptian ones. They continued speaking Hebrew and never informed on each other. These three things gave the Israelites strength to bear the pain of slavery.

תְּפִלּוֹת שַׁבָּת
SHABBAT PRAYERS

תְּפִלּוֹת שַׁבָּת

SHABBAT PRAYERS

The ancient rabbis and sages believed that it was extremely important for Jews to worship together as a united community. They felt that public worship promoted unity, molding separate individuals into a group with shared identity, interests, and goals. At first the Holy Temple in Jerusalem was the central institution for public worship. After the destruction of the Temple, the exiles in Babylon assembled in groups to recite passages from the Torah, observe the festivals and sing psalms. The Hebrew name for this kind of assembly is *Knesset.* It ws translated into Greek as synagogos. Today the synagogue is known by three names, and serves three purposes:

1. בֵּית תְּפִלָּה - House of Worship.
2. בֵּית מִדְרָשׁ - House of Study.
3. בֵּית כְּנֶסֶת - House of Assembly.

Our people have honored Shabbat throughout history. The Talmud tells us that every person, no matter how rich or poor, must personally honor the Sabbath. This section of the text contains some of the prayers which you will recite in the synagogue on Friday night and during Shabbat morning services.

WELCOME IN PEACE

On these two facing pages you will learn to read some of the words and phrases found in

שָׁלוֹם עֲלֵיכֶם

WORD ENDINGS

1 עַל+כֶם = עֲלֵיכֶם   בּוֹא+כֶם = בּוֹאֲכֶם,   צֵאת+כֶם = צֵאתְכֶם.

2 מֶלֶךְ+■ֵי = מַלְכֵי   מַלְאָךְ+■ֵי = מַלְאֲכֵי.

WORD BEGINNINGS

1 הַ+קָדוֹשׁ=הַקָּדוֹשׁ
הַ+מְלָכִים=הַמְּלָכִים,
הַ+שָּׁרֵת=הַשָּׁרֵת.

WORD FAMILY

1 מֶלֶךְ, מַלְכֵי, מְלָכִים.

TEFILLAH PHRASES

1 בָּרוּךְ הוּא, שָׁלוֹם עֲלֵיכֶם, מַלְכֵי הַמְּלָכִים.
2 בּוֹאֲכֶם לְשָׁלוֹם, מַלְאֲכֵי הַשָּׁרֵת, בָּרְכוּנִי לְשָׁלוֹם.

WELCOME IN PEACE

שָׁלוֹם עֲלֵיכֶם contains four stanzas. Only the first line of each stanza is different. Notice that each of these lines contains the word שָׁלוֹם. What special feeling does the word שָׁלוֹם convey to שַׁבָּת?

1 Welcome in peace,	1 שָׁלוֹם עֲלֵיכֶם,
2 O, angels of God,	2 מַלְאֲכֵי הַשָּׁרֵת,
3 Messengers most high,	3 מַלְאֲכֵי עֶלְיוֹן,
4 Sovereign ruler,	4 מִמֶּלֶךְ מַלְכֵי הַמְּלָכִים,
5 Your holiness we glorify.	5 הַקָּדוֹשׁ בָּרוּךְ הוּא.
6 Enter in peace,	6 בּוֹאֲכֶם לְשָׁלוֹם,
7 O, angels of God,	7 מַלְאֲכֵי הַשָּׁרֵת,
8 Messengers most high,	8 מַלְאֲכֵי עֶלְיוֹן,
9 Sovereign ruler,	9 מִמֶּלֶךְ מַלְכֵי הַמְּלָכִים,
10 Your holiness we glorify.	10 הַקָּדוֹשׁ בָּרוּךְ הוּא.
11 Bless us with peace	11 בָּרְכוּנִי לְשָׁלוֹם,
12 O, angels of God,	12 מַלְאֲכֵי הַשָּׁרֵת,
13 Messengers most high,	13 מַלְאֲכֵי עֶלְיוֹן,
14 Sovereign ruler,	14 מִמֶּלֶךְ מַלְכֵי הַמְּלָכִים,
15 Your holiness we glorify.	15 הַקָּדוֹשׁ בָּרוּךְ הוּא.
16 Depart in peace,	16 צֵאתְכֶם לְשָׁלוֹם,
17 O, angels of God,	17 מַלְאֲכֵי הַשָּׁרֵת,
18 Messengers most high,	18 מַלְאֲכֵי עֶלְיוֹן,
19 Sovereign ruler,	19 מִמֶּלֶךְ מַלְכֵי הַמְּלָכִים,
20 Your holiness we glorify.	20 הַקָּדוֹשׁ בָּרוּךְ הוּא.

שָׁלוֹם עֲלֵיכֶם

שָׁלוֹם עֲלֵיכֶם is a short, simple rhythmic greeting for the Angels of God (מַלְאֲכֵי הַשָּׁרֵת) welcoming them into our midst and asking them to bless our homes with peace and happiness.

WELCOMING THE SABBATH

The ceremony of greeting the Sabbath is called Kabballat Shabbat—Welcoming the Shabbat. This ceremony was first introduced by the Kabbalists (religious mystics) of Safed in the 16th century.

On Friday afternoon they dressed in white and paraded to the edge of town to greet the Shabbat Queen. As they waited the mystics sang psalms of welcome and joy. One of their favorite psalms was שָׁלוֹם עֲלֵיכֶם.

The fourth of the Ten Commandment gave something to the world that it never had before—a weekly day of rest, the Shabbat. Before that time, people worked day in and day out, all through the year. No one even thought of a day of rest. The idea of a Day of Rest is a very important Jewish contribution to civilization.

HOW TO RECITE שָׁלוֹם עֲלֵיכֶם

The hymn Shalom Aleichem can be recited in the home before the Kiddush.

It is also one of the opening prayers in the Kabbalat Shabbat service on Friday night.

Each of the four stanzas is recited three times.

The custom of reciting שָׁלוֹם עֲלֵיכֶם is based on the Talmudic legend that two angels accompany every Jew when he or she returns from Friday evening services. One angel is dressed in white with a sweet smile. The other angel has an angry face. When they reach the house, both angels rush ahead and peek inside. If the people who live there are not ready to meet the Sabbath Queen—the angry angel claps his hands in glee. "Ha!" he cries, "May all the Sabbaths of this family be like this!"

And the sweet angel, much as he dislikes it, must say "Amen." But, if there is a special Shabbat glow, and a spirit of warmth fills every nook and cranny of the house, the angry angel slinks away, while the sweet Angel laughs, flutters his wings and says "Ah, may all your Sabbaths be like this one!" Now the grumpy angel is forced to say "Amen".

HAPPY ARE THOSE

On these two facing pages you will learn to read some of the words and phrases found in אַשְׁרֵי.

WORD ENDINGS

1	בַּיִת+ךָ=בֵּיתְךָ	אֲבָרֵךְ+ךָ=אֲבָרְכֶךָ.
2	אֲרֹמֵם+ךָ=אֲרֹמִמְךָ	שֵׁם+ךָ=שִׁמְךָ, מַלְכוּת+ךָ=מַלְכוּתְךָ, מֶמְשֶׁלֶת+ךָ=מֶמְשַׁלְתְּךָ.
3	חֲסִידִים+ךָ=חֲסִידֶיךָ	גְּבוּרֹת+ךָ=גְּבוּרֹתֶיךָ, נִפְלְאֹת+ךָ=נִפְלְאֹתֶיךָ, נוֹרְאוֹת+ךָ=נוֹרְאוֹתֶיךָ, מַעֲשִׂים+ךָ=מַעֲשֶׂיךָ.
4	גְּדֻלָּה+וֹ=גְּדֻלָּתוֹ	מַלְכוּת+וֹ=מַלְכוּתוֹ.
5	רַחֲמִים+■ָיו=רַחֲמָיו	מַעֲשִׂים +■ָיו=מַעֲשָׂיו, גְּבוּרֹת+■ָיו=גְּבוּרֹתָיו.
6	יֹאמַר+וּ=יֹאמְרוּ	יַבִּיעַ+וּ=יַבִּיעוּ, יַגִּיד+וּ=יַגִּידוּ, יְדַבֵּר+וּ=יְדַבְּרוּ.

WORD BEGINNINGS

1 | לְ+עוֹלָם=לְעוֹלָם | לְ+דוֹר=לְדוֹר, לְ+הוֹדִיעַ=לְהוֹדִיעַ.

2 | וַ+אֲבָרְכָה=וַאֲבָרְכָה | וַ+אֲהַלְלָה=וַאֲהַלְלָה, וַ+חֲסִידֶיךָ=וַחֲסִידֶיךָ.

3 | וְ+דִבְרֵי=וְדִבְרֵי | וְ+לִגְדֻלָּתוֹ=וְלִגְדֻלָּתוֹ, וְ+צִדְקָתְךָ=וְצִדְקָתְךָ,
וְ+רַחֲמָיו=וְרַחֲמָיו.

4 | וּ+כְבוֹד=וּכְבוֹד | וּ+גְבוּרֹתֶיךָ=וּגְבוּרֹתֶיךָ, וּ+מְהֻלָּל=וּמְהֻלָּל,
וּ+גְדֻלָּתְךָ=וּגְדֻלָּתְךָ, וּ+גְדָל=וּגְדָל,
וּ+מֶמְשַׁלְתְּךָ=וּמֶמְשַׁלְתְּךָ.

5 | הַ+מֶּלֶךְ=הַמֶּלֶךְ | הַ+עָם=הָעָם, הַ+אָדָם=הָאָדָם.

WORD FAMILIES

1 חֶסֶד, חֲסִידֶיךָ. אֱלֹהִים, אֱלֹהָיו, אֱלֹהֵי.

2 בָּרוּךְ, אֲבָרְכָה, אֲבָרְכֶךָ, יְבָרְכוּכָה.

3 תְּהִלָּה, מְהֻלָּל, אֲהַלְלָה. גָּדוֹל, גְּדֻלָּתוֹ, גְּדָל.

TEFILLAH PHRASES

1 יוֹשְׁבֵי בֵיתֶךָ, אַשְׁרֵי הָעָם, תְּהִלָּה לְדָוִד, וַאֲבָרְכָה שִׁמְךָ.

2 וַאֲהַלְלָה שִׁמְךָ, גָּדוֹל יְיָ, וּגְבוּרֹתֶיךָ יַגִּידוּ, וּגְדֻלָּתְךָ אֲסַפְּרֶנָּה.

3 וְצִדְקָתְךָ יְרַנֵּנוּ, חַנּוּן וְרַחוּם יְיָ, וּגְדָל חָסֶד, טוֹב יְיָ לַכֹּל.

HAPPY ARE THOSE

אַשְׁרֵי consists of Psalm 145, plus two introductory verses from other psalms. It is read twice during the שַׁחֲרִית service and once during the מוּסָף service. Notice the alphabetic acrostic.

1. Happy are those who dwell in Your house,	1 אַשְׁרֵי יוֹשְׁבֵי בֵיתֶךָ,
2. May they continue to praise You, Selah.	2 עוֹד יְהַלְלוּךָ סֶּלָה.
3. Happy are the people that are so situated.	3 אַשְׁרֵי הָעָם שֶׁכָּכָה לוֹ,
4. Happy are the people for whom Adonai is their God.	4 אַשְׁרֵי הָעָם שֶׁיְיָ אֱלֹהָיו.
5. A hymn of praise by David.	5 תְּהִלָּה לְדָוִד:
6. I will praise You, my God, the Ruler.	6 אֲרוֹמִמְךָ אֱלוֹהַי הַמֶּלֶךְ
7. I will bless Your name for ever and ever.	7 וַאֲבָרְכָה שִׁמְךָ לְעוֹלָם וָעֶד.
8. Every day I will bless You.	8 בְּכָל יוֹם אֲבָרְכֶךָּ,
9. I will praise Your name for ever and ever.	9 וַאֲהַלְלָה שִׁמְךָ לְעוֹלָם וָעֶד.
10. Adonai is great and highly praised,	10 גָּדוֹל יְיָ וּמְהֻלָּל מְאֹד,
11. God's greatness is unknowable.	11 וְלִגְדֻלָּתוֹ* אֵין חֵקֶר.
12. Generation after generation will praise Your deeds;	12 דּוֹר לְדוֹר יְשַׁבַּח מַעֲשֶׂיךָ,
13. They will retell Your mighty doings.	13 וּגְבוּרֹתֶיךָ יַגִּידוּ.
14. The splendor of Your glorious majesty	14 הֲדַר כְּבוֹד הוֹדֶךָ,
15. And Your miraculous deeds I will recount;	15 וְדִבְרֵי נִפְלְאֹתֶיךָ אָשִׂיחָה.
16. They tell of Your awesome might	16 וֶעֱזוּז נוֹרְאוֹתֶיךָ יֹאמֵרוּ,
17. And tell of Your greatness.	17 וּגְדֻלָּתְךָ אֲסַפְּרֶנָּה
18. They proclaim a reminder of Your great goodness	18 זֵכֶר רַב טוּבְךָ יַבִּיעוּ,
19. And sing of Your rightousness.	19 וְצִדְקָתְךָ יְרַנֵּנוּ.

20. Adonai is gracious and merciful,	חַנּוּן וְרַחוּם יְיָ, 20
21. Slow to anger and filled with great kindness.	אֶרֶךְ אַפַּיִם וּגְדָל חָסֶד. 21
22. Adonai is good to all,	טוֹב יְיָ לַכָּל, 22
23. And God's mercy is over all creations.	וְרַחֲמָיו עַל כָּל מַעֲשָׂיו*. 23
24. Your creations will thank you, Adonai.	יוֹדוּךָ יְיָ כָּל מַעֲשֶׂיךָ, 24
25. Your followers will bless You.	וַחֲסִידֶיךָ יְבָרְכוּכָה. 25
26. They speak of Your glorious kingdom	כְּבוֹד מַלְכוּתְךָ יֹאמֵרוּ 26
27. And speak of Your might,	וּגְבוּרָתְךָ יְדַבֵּרוּ. 27
28. To tell all people Your mighty deeds	לְהוֹדִיעַ לִבְנֵי הָאָדָם גְּבוּרֹתָיו*, 28
29. And the glorious splendor of Your kingship.	וּכְבוֹד הֲדַר מַלְכוּתוֹ. 29
30. Your kingdom is forever,	מַלְכוּתְךָ, מַלְכוּת כָּל עוֹלָמִים, 30
31. Your rule is for generation after generation	וּמֶמְשַׁלְתְּךָ בְּכָל דֹּר וָדֹר. 31
32. God supports all who fall,	סוֹמֵךְ יְיָ לְכָל הַנֹּפְלִים, 32
33. And lifts up all those who are oppressed.	וְזוֹקֵף לְכָל הַכְּפוּפִים. 33

The remainder of the prayer after the letter ס has been omitted.
The letter נ is not found in the prayer. See the comment on page 74.

Why did the rabbis decide that אַשְׁרֵי should be recited 3 times a day?

Some scholars believe it was because the word אַשְׁרֵי is repeated three times in the introductory sentence of the prayer.

אַשְׁרֵי is recited after the Haftarah reading and when the Torah is returned to the Ark. The conclusion of the תּוֹרָה service also begins with the recitation of אַשְׁרֵי.

The אַשְׁרֵי prayer is taken from the Book of Psalms. This beautiful prayer is said to have been written by King David. When the Levites in the ancient Temple sang the אַשְׁרֵי, they were accompanied by the music of stringed instruments, flutes, and cymbals.

The first letter of אַשְׁרֵי is an א, the first letter of the alefbet. Notice that line 8 starts with a ב, the second letter of the alefbet. All of the letters of the alefbet are contained in the אַשְׁרֵי acrostic, except the letter נ. Some scholars believe that the נ is deleted since it stands for the Hebrew word נְפִילָה, which means "fallen." This refers to the falling and destruction of the First and Second Temples.

In 1993, Professor Avraham Biran discovered the first commemorative stone inscription ever found that mentions the House of David and the king of Israel. This ninth-century B.C.E. stela was uncovered at the excavations at Tel Dan near the Lebanese border. The inscription on the stone consists of thirteen broken lines of Aramaic text.

אַשְׁרֵי is the only psalm which is labeled as a תְּהִילָּה. The Hebrew title of the Book of Psalms is תְּהִלִּים. The word תְּהִלִּים is derived from the word תְּהִילָּה.

When you take a train or a plane, you are putting your safety in the hands of an unknown pilot or engineer you have never seen. Millions of travelers do the same thing every day of the year.

Think of how much more sense it makes to put your life in the hands of God, who created the world and has guided it through eons of years.

SYNAGOGUE DUTIES

Over the centuries certain synagogue duties have been performed by persons specially trained in Jewish law, customs, and traditions. Here are a few of the officers of the synagogue and brief descriptions of their history and the role they play today.

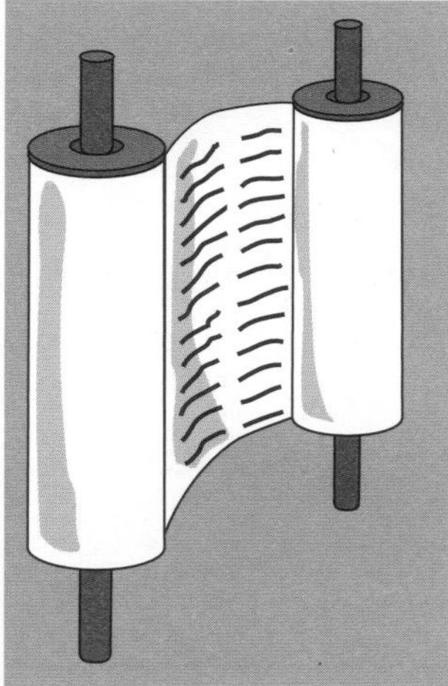

רַבִּי

This title, which means "my teacher," is given to a religious leader and teacher. The title was first used during the time of the destruction of the Temple (70 C.E.). Today, most rabbis are ordained by a rabbinical seminary from which they graduate. The duties of the rabbi are to serve as religious leader of the congregation; make decisions on practical questions of Jewish law; conduct services and preach on Sabbaths, holy days, and festivals; teach Judaism to children and adult groups, officiate at important events in the life of the congregants (such as circumcision, Bar/Bat Mitzvah, marriage, and burial).

חַזָּן

In the days of the Mishnah and the Talmud, the חַזָּן (hazzan) was the caretaker of the synagogue and an official at religous ceremonies. Today, the חַזָּן, usually called the cantor in English, is someone who chants the services in the synagogue. In some synagogues the cantor also leads the choir and teaches religious classes.

בַּעַל קוֹרֵא

The בַּעַל קוֹרֵא ("master reader") chants the fixed portions (sidrot) from the Torah.

שַׁמָּשׁ

The שַׁמָּשׁ (sexton) has had a role in synagogue life for many centuries. In early times he was the superintendent of the synagogue and in East European towns would call the congregants to services every morning at dawn. Today the שַׁמָּשׁ helps the רַבִּי with the synagogue duties.

גַּבַּאי

The title גַּבַּאי comes from the Hebrew word for "to collect." In medieval times the גַּבַּאי was a very important congregational official, for he was the treasurer of the synagogue. Today, the גַּבַּאי is often a congregant who is given certain synagogue duties to perform.

בַּעַל תּוֹקֵעַ

The בַּעַל תּוֹקֵעַ ("master blower") blows the shofar when synagogue services require it, such as on Rosh Hashanah and Yom Kippur.

בַּעַל תְּפִלָּה

The בַּעַל תְּפִלָּה is a person other than the חַזָּן who leads the congregation in prayer.

HEAR, O ISRAEL

On these two facing pages some of the words and phrases found in the first section of the שְׁמַע יִשְׂרָאֵל.

WORD ENDINGS

1 אָהַב + תָּ = אָהַבְתָּ

דִּבֵּר + תָּ = דִּבַּרְתָּ.

2 אֱלֹהִים + ■ֶיךָ = אֱלֹהֶיךָ

מְאֹד■ֶיךָ = מְאֹדֶךָ, לֵבָב + ■ֶיךָ = לְבָבֶךָ,

3 בַּיִת + ■ֶךָ = בֵּיתֶךָ

קוּם + ■ֶךָ = קוּמֶךָ, לֵבָב + ■ְךָ = לְבָבְךָ

יָד + ■ֶךָ = יָדֶךָ, נֶפֶשׁ + ■ְךָ = נַפְשְׁךָ,

4 מִצְוָה + ■ְךָ = מְצַוְּךָ

שֶׁבֶת + ■ְךָ = שִׁבְתְּךָ, שְׁכֹב + ■ְךָ = שָׁכְבְּךָ,

לֶכֶת + ■ְךָ = לֶכְתְּךָ, עַיִן + ■ֶיךָ = עֵינֶיךָ,

שַׁעַר + ■ֶיךָ = שְׁעָרֶיךָ, בֵּן + ■ֶיךָ = בָּנֶיךָ.

5 כְּתַבְתָּ + ם = כְּתַבְתָּם

קְשַׁרְתָּ + ם = קְשַׁרְתָּם.

WORD BEGINNINGS

1 לְ+עוֹלָם = לְעוֹלָם   לְ+טֹטָפֹת = לְטֹטָפֹת,   וְ+אָהַבְתָּ = וְאָהַבְתָּ,

לְ+אוֹת = לְאוֹת,   לְ+בָּנֶיךָ = לְבָנֶיךָ.

2 בְּ+כָל = בְּכָל   בְּ+שִׁבְתְּךָ = בְּשִׁבְתְּךָ,   בְּ+בֵיתֶךָ = בְּבֵיתֶךָ.

3 וּ+בְכָל = וּבְכָל   וּ+בְּשָׁכְבְּךָ = וּבְשָׁכְבְּךָ,   וּ+בְקוּמֶךָ = וּבְקוּמֶךָ,

וּ+קְשַׁרְתָּם = וּקְשַׁרְתָּם,   וּ+כְתַבְתָּם = וּכְתַבְתָּם,

וּ+בִשְׁעָרֶיךָ = וּבִשְׁעָרֶיךָ,   וּ+בְלֶכְתְּךָ = וּבְלֶכְתְּךָ.

4 הַ+דְּבָרִים = הַדְּבָרִים   הָ+אֵלֶּה = הָאֵלֶּה,   הַ+יּוֹם = הַיּוֹם.

5 וְ+הָיוּ = וְהָיוּ   וְ+דִבַּרְתָּ = וְדִבַּרְתָּ,   וְ+שִׁנַּנְתָּם = וְשִׁנַּנְתָּם,

וְ+אָהַבְתָּ = וְאָהַבְתָּ.

WORD FAMILIES

1 אֱלֹהֵינוּ אֱלֹהֶיךָ. בְּכָל וּבְכָל.

2 הָיוּ וְהָיוּ. בְּבֵיתֶךָ בֵּיתֶךָ.

TEFILLAH PHRASES

1 מְזֻזוֹת בֵּיתֶךָ,   בְּכָל לְבָבְךָ,   יְיָ אֱלֹהֶיךָ,   בְּשִׁבְתְּךָ בְּבֵיתֶךָ.

2 וְהָיוּ הַדְּבָרִים,   עַל לְבָבֶךָ,   וּבְשָׁכְבְּךָ וּבְקוּמֶךָ,   וּקְשַׁרְתָּם לְאוֹת.

3 וְהָיוּ לְטֹטָפֹת,   וּבְכָל מְאֹדֶךָ,   מְצַוְּךָ הַיּוֹם,   שְׁמַע יִשְׂרָאֵל.

HEAR, O ISRAEL

The שְׁמַע יִשְׂרָאֵל consists of three passages from the Torah. The first section of the שְׁמַע יִשְׂרָאֵל is from Deuteronomy 6:4–8. Notice that the first letters of the word אֵל מֶלֶךְ נֶאֱמָן make up the word אָמֵן.

When praying alone add: אֵל מֶלֶךְ נֶאֱמָן

1. Hear, O Israel	1 שְׁמַע יִשְׂרָאֵל,
2. Adonai is our God,	2 יְיָ אֱלֹהֵינוּ,
3. Adonai is One.	3 יְיָ אֶחָד.
4. Blessed is the name of God's glorious kingdom,	4 בָּרוּךְ שֵׁם כְּבוֹד מַלְכוּתוֹ,
5. Forever and ever.	5 לְעוֹלָם וָעֶד.
6. And you shall love Adonai your God,	6 וְאָהַבְתָּ אֵת יְיָ אֱלֹהֶיךָ,
7. With all your heart,	7 בְּכָל לְבָבְךָ,
8. And with all your soul,	8 וּבְכָל נַפְשְׁךָ,
9. And with all your possessions.	9 וּבְכָל מְאֹדֶךָ.
10. And these things,	10 וְהָיוּ הַדְּבָרִים הָאֵלֶּה,
11. Which I command you today,	11 אֲשֶׁר אָנֹכִי מְצַוְּךָ הַיּוֹם,
12. Shall be on your heart,	12 עַל לְבָבֶךָ,
13. And you shall teach them to your children,	13 וְשִׁנַּנְתָּם לְבָנֶיךָ,
14. And you shall speak of them,	14 וְדִבַּרְתָּ בָּם,
15. When you sit in your home,	15 בְּשִׁבְתְּךָ בְּבֵיתֶךָ,
16. And when you walk in the street,	16 וּבְלֶכְתְּךָ בַדֶּרֶךְ,
17. When you lie down and when you get up,	17 וּבְשָׁכְבְּךָ וּבְקוּמֶךָ,
18. And you shall tie them	18 וּקְשַׁרְתָּם

19. As a sign upon your hand,	19 לְאוֹת עַל יָדֶךָ,
20. And they shall be as frontlets	20 וְהָיוּ לְטֹטָפֹת
21. Between your eyes.	21 בֵּין עֵינֶיךָ.
22. And you shall write them	22 וּכְתַבְתָּם
23. On the doorposts of your home,	23 עַל מְזֻזוֹת בֵּיתֶךָ
24. And inside your gates.	24 וּבִשְׁעָרֶיךָ.

HEAR, O ISRAEL שְׁמַע יִשְׂרָאֵל

The rabbis say that the word מְאֹדֶךָ (9) refers to "your possessions." In other words, we are commanded to use our possessions to help people and institutions which are in need. "Your possessions" can be a toy for a needy child, or help for a student who needs tutoring, or giving money for a good cause.

The שְׁמַע says, "and you shall bind them for a sign upon your hand, and they shall be frontlets between your eyes." This commandment refers to the תְּפִלִּין.

The תְּפִלִּין are two small leather boxes with attached leather straps. The straps are to be wrapped around the head and arm to hold them in place. Inside each of the leather boxes are handwritten parchments with quotations from the Torah. Traditional Jews wear the תְּפִלִּין during the morning prayer service. Among Traditional and Conservative Jews, it is customary to start putting on תְּפִלִּין at the age of thirteen.

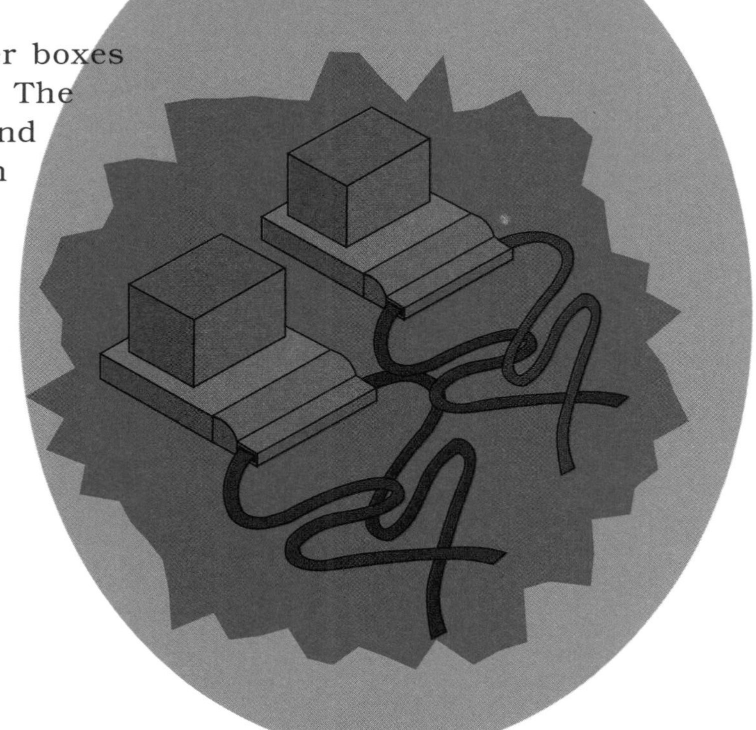

The seeds of knowledge and ideas being planted in you today by your rabbi and your teachers are the thought and actions which will grow in you tomorrow. The ideas of loving God, Torah study, doing Mitzvot and freedom from slavery are the seeds for a happy meaningful Jewish life.

It is for you to take these ideas and talk about them - וְדִבַּרְתָּ בָּם *- when you sit in your house -* בְּשִׁבְתְּךָ בְּבֵיתֶךָ *-, when you bike on the road -* בְּלֶכְתְּךָ בַדֶּרֶךְ *- when you lie down -* בְּשָׁכְבְּךָ *- and when you get up,* בְּקוּמֶךָ.

Your rabbi, your teachers and your parents have helped plant these seeds. As you grow older, it will become your turn to nourish these tiny seeds with new ideas and positive Jewish actions.

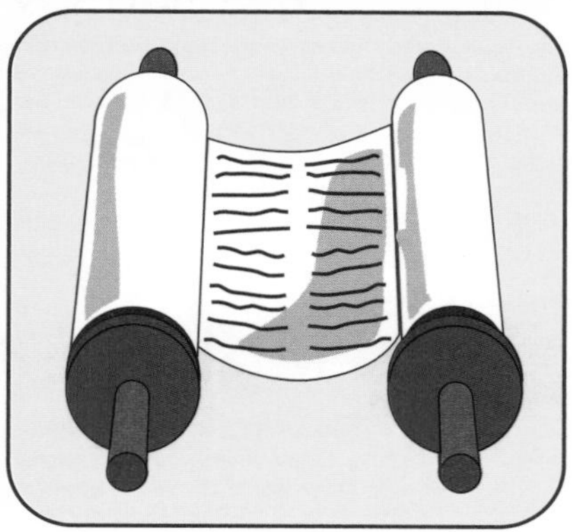

The three paragraphs of the שְׁמַע contain a total of 245 words. The Sages added three words, אֵל מֶלֶךְ נֶאֱמָן, making the total 248. There are exactly 248 positive commandments in the Torah. According to the Talmud, there are 613 commandments in the Torah; 248 of them are positive and 365 are negative.

In the Torah, the last letter of the word שְׁמַע, the ע, and the last letter of אֶחָד, the ד, are written larger than the other letters. These two large letters form the word עֵד, meaning "witness." Every Jew reciting the שְׁמַע becomes one of the God's witnesses, testifying to God's oneness.

שמע ישראל יהוה אלהינו יהוה אחד

בְּכָל נַפְשְׁךָ (8)

The rabbis explained that the phrase בְּכָל נַפְשְׁךָ ("with all your soul") means to love God with your life and your last drop of blood.
Rabbi Akiba lived in the second century, when the Romans ruled Jerusalem. He was a leader and a great rabbi. Rabbi Akiba joined Bar Kokhba in a rebellion against the Romans. When the rebellion failed, Rabbi Akiba, who was arrested while studying the Torah, was tortured to death. As he died he recited the words of the שְׁמַע with his last breath. Since that time many Jews who are near death have tried to recite the שְׁמַע as their last words.

HOW TO RECITE THE שְׁמַע

Some people recite the שְׁמַע in a special way. They grasp the four צִיצִת of their talit in their left hand. Then they close their eyes as they recite the first 6 words (lines 1,2,3 in the prayer). Closing their eyes helps them to concentrate their thoughts on the prayer.

AND IF YOU LISTEN

On these two facing pages, you will learn to read some of the words and phrases that are found in the second part of the prayer שְׁמַע יִשְׂרָאֵל.

WORD ENDINGS

1 | אָבֹת+כֶם=אֲבֹתֵיכֶם |

בָּנִים+כֶם=בְּנֵיכֶם,   לֵבַב+כֶם=לְבַבְכֶם,

עֵינַיִם+כֶם=עֵינֵיכֶם,   יָמִים+כֶם=יְמֵיכֶם,

נֶפֶשׁ+כֶם=נַפְשְׁכֶם,   יָד+כֶם=יֶדְכֶם.

2 | סָר+תֶּם=סַרְתֶּם |

עָבַד+תֶּם=עֲבַדְתֶּם,   לָמַד+תֶּם=לְמַדְתֶּם,

שָׂם+תֶּם=שַׂמְתֶּם .

3 | מְזוּזָה+וֹת=מְזוּזוֹת |

טוֹטֶפֶת+וֹת=טוֹטָפֹת .

4 | מְהֵר+■ָה=מְהֵרָה, |

טֹב+■ָה=טֹבָה .

5 | שֶׁבֶת+ךָ=שִׁבְתְּךָ |

בַּיִת+ךָ=בֵּיתֶךָ,   שְׁכֹב+ךָ=שָׁכְבְּךָ,

לֶכֶת+ךָ=לֶכְתְּךָ,   קוּם+ךָ=קוּמֶךָ,

שְׁעָרִים+ךָ=שְׁעָרֶיךָ.

WORD BEGINNINGS

1 | וְ+סַרְתֶּם=וְסַרְתֶּם | וְ+הִשְׁתַּחֲוִיתֶם=וְהִשְׁתַּחֲוִיתֶם,

וְ+חָרָה=וְחָרָה, וְ+שַׂמְתֶּם=וְשַׂמְתֶּם,

וְ+עָצַר=וְעָצַר, וְ+לִמַּדְתֶּם=וְלִמַּדְתֶּם,

וְ+הָיוּ=וְהָיוּ, וְ+עַל=וְעַל, וְ+לֹא=וְלֹא.

2 | לְ+אוֹת=לְאוֹת | לְ+טוֹטָפֹת=לְטוֹטָפֹת, לְ+דַבֵּר=לְדַבֵּר,

לְ+מַעַן=לְמַעַן.

3 | וּ+כְתַבְתָּם=וּכְתַבְתָּם | וּ+בְקוּמֶךָ=וּבְקוּמֶךָ, וּ+בִשְׁעָרֶיךָ=וּבִשְׁעָרֶיךָ,

וּ+קְשַׁרְתֶּם=וּקְשַׁרְתֶּם, וּ+בְלֶכְתְּךָ=וּבְלֶכְתְּךָ.

4 | הַ+אֲדָמָה=הָאֲדָמָה | הַ+טֹּבָה= הַטֹּבָה, הַ+שָּׁמַיִם=הַשָּׁמַיִם,

הַ+אֶרֶץ=הָאָרֶץ.

5 | בְּ+שִׁבְתְּךָ=בְּשִׁבְתְּךָ | בְּ+בֵיתֶךָ=בְּבֵיתֶךָ, בְּ+לֶכְתְּךָ=בְּלֶכְתְּךָ,

בְּ+שָׁכְבְּךָ=בְּשָׁכְבְּךָ, בְּ+קוּמֶךָ=בְּקוּמֶךָ.

TEFILLAH PHRASES

1 הִשָּׁמְרוּ לָכֶם, לְאוֹת עַל יֶדְכֶם, לְדַבֵּר בָּם, וְעַל נַפְשְׁכֶם.

2 בְּשִׁבְתְּךָ בְּבֵיתֶךָ, וְלִמַּדְתֶּם אֹתָם, וְעָצַר אֶת הַשָּׁמַיִם.

3 עַל לְבַבְכֶם, בֵּין עֵינֵיכֶם, אֲשֶׁר נִשְׁבַּע יְיָ, וּקְשַׁרְתֶּם אֹתָם.

4 וַאֲבַדְתֶּם מְהֵרָה, בֵּיתֶךָ וּבִשְׁעָרֶיךָ, עַל הָאֲדָמָה, וְחָרָה אַף יְיָ.

AND IF YOU LISTEN

The second section of the שְׁמַע יִשְׂרָאֵל is found in the fifth book of the Torah, Deuteronomy 11:13–21.

1. And if you listen	1 וְהָיָה אִם שָׁמֹעַ תִּשְׁמְעוּ
2. To My Mitzvot,	2 אֶל מִצְוֹתַי,
3. Which I command you today,	3 אֲשֶׁר אָנֹכִי מְצַוֶּה אֶתְכֶם הַיּוֹם,
4. To love and serve Adonai your God	4 לְאַהֲבָה אֶת יְיָ אֱלֹהֵיכֶם וּלְעָבְדוֹ,
5. With all your heart and with all your soul;	5 בְּכָל לְבַבְכֶם וּבְכָל נַפְשְׁכֶם:
6. And I shall send rain on your land in its season	6 וְנָתַתִּי מְטַר אַרְצְכֶם בְּעִתּוֹ,
7. The autumn rain and the spring rain,	7 יוֹרֶה וּמַלְקוֹשׁ,
8. And you shall harvest your grain,	8 וְאָסַפְתָּ דְגָנֶךָ
9. Your wine, and your oil,	9 וְתִירשְׁךָ וְיִצְהָרֶךָ:
10. And I shall provide grass	10 וְנָתַתִּי עֵשֶׂב
11. In your field for your cattle	11 בְּשָׂדְךָ לִבְהֶמְתֶּךָ,
12. And you shall eat and be satisfied.	12 וְאָכַלְתָּ וְשָׂבָעְתָּ:
13. Be careful,	13 הִשָּׁמְרוּ לָכֶם
14. Lest your hearts will be fooled,	14 פֶּן יִפְתֶּה לְבַבְכֶם,
15 And you turn away	15 וְסַרְתֶּם
16. To worship other gods,	16 וַעֲבַדְתֶּם אֱלֹהִים אֲחֵרִים
17. And bow down to them	17 וְהִשְׁתַּחֲוִיתֶם לָהֶם.
18. And Adonai will be angry with you	18 וְחָרָה אַף יְיָ בָּכֶם,
19. And will shut the heavens,	19 וְעָצַר אֶת הַשָּׁמַיִם
20. And there will be no rain,	20 וְלֹא יִהְיֶה מָטָר,
21. And the earth will not give (grow) its food,	21 וְהָאֲדָמָה לֹא תִתֵּן אֶת יְבוּלָהּ,
22. And you will swiftly disappear	22 וַאֲבַדְתֶּם מְהֵרָה
23. From the good earth	23 מֵעַל הָאָרֶץ הַטֹּבָה,

24. Which Adonai gives you.	24 אֲשֶׁר יְיָ נֹתֵן לָכֶם.
25. And you shall place these words	25 וְשַׂמְתֶּם אֶת דְּבָרַי אֵלֶּה
26. On your heart,	26 עַל לְבַבְכֶם,
27. And on your soul,	27 וְעַל נַפְשְׁכֶם,
28. And you shall tie them	28 וּקְשַׁרְתֶּם אֹתָם
29. As a sign upon your hands,	29 לְאוֹת עַל יֶדְכֶם,
30. And they shall be as frontlets	30 וְהָיוּ לְטוֹטָפֹת
31. Between your eyes,	31 בֵּין עֵינֵיכֶם,
32. And you shall teach them to your children,	32 וְלִמַּדְתֶּם אֹתָם אֶת בְּנֵיכֶם,
33. And speak of them,	33 לְדַבֵּר בָּם,
34. While seated in your home,	34 בְּשִׁבְתְּךָ בְּבֵיתֶךָ,
35. And when you go on a journey,	35 וּבְלֶכְתְּךָ בַדֶּרֶךְ,
36. When you lie down and when you get up.	36 וּבְשָׁכְבְּךָ וּבְקוּמֶךָ.
37. And you shall write them	37 וּכְתַבְתָּם
38. On the doorposts of your home	38 עַל מְזוּזוֹת בֵּיתֶךָ
39. And on your gates.	39 וּבִשְׁעָרֶיךָ.
40. So that your days will be many	40 לְמַעַן יִרְבּוּ יְמֵיכֶם
41. And the days of your children upon the earth,	41 וִימֵי בְנֵיכֶם עַל הָאֲדָמָה,
42. Which Adonai swore	42 אֲשֶׁר נִשְׁבַּע יְיָ
43. To give to your ancestors,	43 לַאֲבֹתֵיכֶם לָתֵת לָהֶם,
44. As long as the heavens are above the earth.	44 כִּימֵי הַשָּׁמַיִם עַל הָאָרֶץ.

I WILL SEND RAIN (6) וְנָתַתִּי מְטַר

Ancient Israel was an agricultural country. The farmers depended upon the rains to water the crops בְּעִתּוֹ ("in time"). If the rain did not come in time the whole crop could be ruined. Famine would follow if there was not enough rain for one or two seasons in a row. Thus there was always the problem of how to save the rain, which often came all at once and was not spread over the whole year.

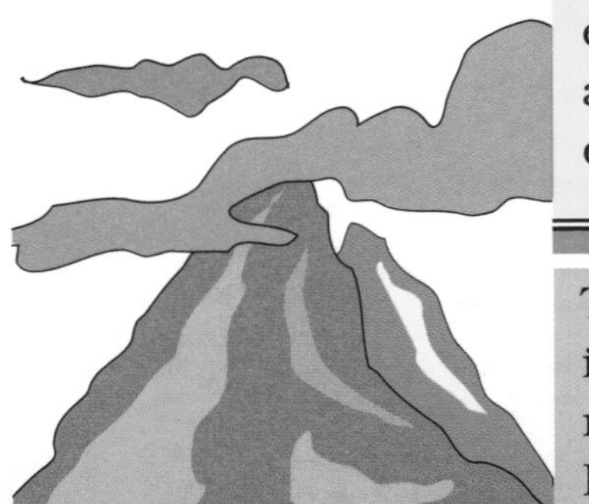

The Nabateans were an ancient people who were very good at saving rain water. For hundreds of years, the Negev lay idle and neglected, a playground for fierce desert winds and sun. Then the Nabateans arrived. A desert people, the Nabateans knew how to survive in the Negev. They knew how to trap and save water. They built dams that stored water during the rainy seasons for use in dry times. The Nabatean civilization ended with the rise of Islam. From that time until the rise of the State of Israel many centuries later, the Negev was again left to the mercy of the desert. In 1890 the pioneers (chalutzim) started returning to Israel. They knew they would have many years of hard work to bring the land back to life. The chalutzim built more dams, dug more wells, drained the water from the swamps—-and the land began to blossom and come to life. Today the modern State of Israel is a beautiful, fertile place. Golden oranges hang from the trees and huge clusters of grapes hang from the vines.The Israelis are now more skilled as farmers than ever before. The Israeli government sends farm experts to poorer countries. The experts from Israel live with the people and teach them better ways to farm. Thus Israel shares with its fellow nations and helps make the world a better and more beautiful place in which to live.

כַּוָּנָה

Did you ever wonder when the great Jewish laws were written down? Not just a few years ago, but centuries ago. In those long-ago times, Jews cared very deeply about the old, the sick, and the helpless. So they followed rules for living that would protect people and make sure justice would be done. Our rabbis teach us that these rules are called מִצְוֹת. In the Torah there are 613 מִצְוֹת. These rules are of two different kinds. One kind is called YES, DO (positive) מִצְוֹת, and the other is called NO, DO NOT (negative) מִצְוֹת. There are 248 postive מִצְוֹת. Positive מִצְוֹת are called מִצְוֹת עֲשֵׂה. The 365 negative מִצְוֹת, are called מִצְוֹת לֹא תַעֲשֶׂה. If we want to live in a holy way, then we must do God's will by observing מִצְוֹת. At the same time that we do God's will, we also help ourselves. It is a מִצְוָה to pray. You know how it helps just to talk things over with your parents or friends. It helps even more to talk to God. Prayer is a מִצְוָה that makes us feel better inside ourselves. You might not know it, but study is a מִצְוָה too, and a very important one. Parents and teachers used to give children honey cakes or drops of honey on the day their studies began. This showed the children that the study of the Torah is sweet and encouraged them to learn.

THE MEZUZAH מְזוּזָה

The מְזוּזָה is a handwritten parchment scroll containing the passage "Write them on the doorposts of your house and your gates." The parchment is enclosed in a decorative holder and is affixed to the right-hand doorpost of a Jewish house.

A small opening is left in the holder with the word שַׁדַּי. The opening allows the parchment to be seen. Some people say that the word שַׁדַּי is made up of the first letters of the Hebrew phrase שׁוֹמֵר דְּלָתוֹת יִשְׂרָאֵל "Guardian of the doors of Israel."

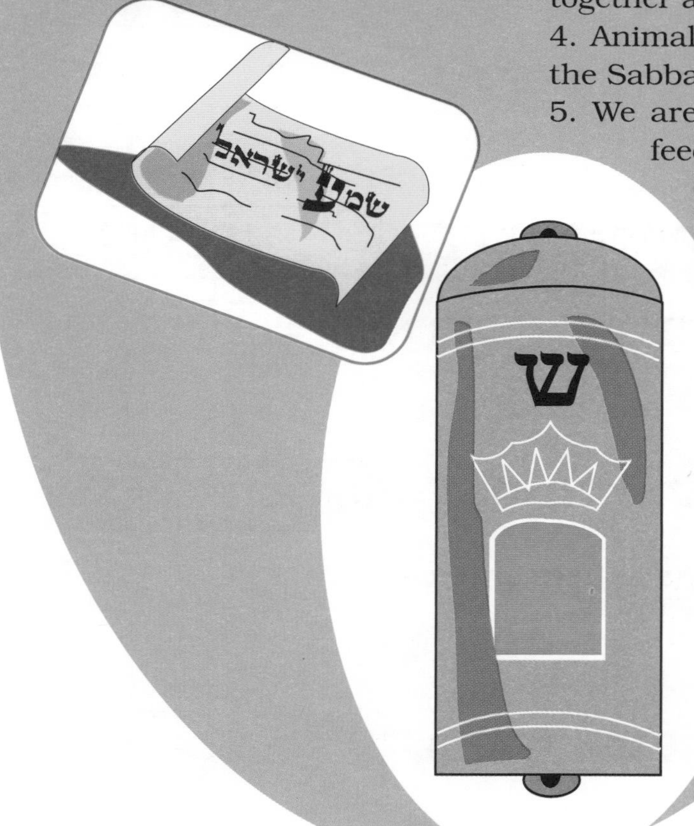

32. "Teach them to your children."

This means that it is important for parents to take time from their busy schedules and supervise the education of their children.

FOR THE GOOD OF ANIMALS

Notice that on line 11 the Torah says "I will provide grass for your cattle." In line 12 the Torah says "you will eat and be satisfied." From these two statements our rabbis deduced that we should first take care of our animals and feed them before eating our own meals. Jews have a long tradition of being kind to animals. Not only are we forbidden to be cruel to animals, but we have laws to protect them—-sort of a Ten Commandments for the Good of Animals.

1. An animal that falls down must be raised with care.
2. An animal working to tread out corn must be allowed to eat from the grain.
3. Animals of different species, like an ox and ass, must not be yoked together for work. Since they have different strengths, it is cruel to force them to work together as if they were equal.
4. Animals must be allowed to rest from working on the Sabbath, just as the owner has to rest.
5. We are not allowed to sit down to a meal before feeding our animals or pets.
6. We are not allowed to make an animal carry a heavier load than it can bear.
7. We are not allowed to abuse an animal.
8. We may not buy any animal or bird unless we can provide enough food for it.
9. Killing animals for sport is forbidden.
10. In slaughtering animals or birds for food, we must try not to cause unnecessary pain. The Jewish laws of Shechitah are designed to keep animals from suffering when meat is prepared for eating.

When a מְזוּזָה is first placed on a Jewish home we recite a special prayer. Some people celebrate with a special ceremony called Hanukat Habayit ("dedication of a new home").

AND GOD SPOKE

On these two facing pages you will learn to read some of the words and phrases found in the third part of the שְׁמַע יִשְׂרָאֵל.

WORD ENDINGS

1 אֶל+הֶם = אֲלֵהֶם

בְּגָדִים+הֶם = בִּגְדֵיהֶם, אַחֲרֵי+הֶם = אַחֲרֵיהֶם.

2 אֶת+כֶם = אֶתְכֶם

לֵבָב+כֶם = לְבַבְכֶם, אֱלֹהִים+כֶם = אֱלֹהֵיכֶם,

עֵינַיִם+כֶם = עֵינֵיכֶם.

3 נָתַן+וּ = נָתְנוּ

תָּתוּר+וּ = תָתוּרוּ, עָשָׂה+וּ = עָשׂוּ,

תִּזְכֹּר+וּ = תִּזְכְּרוּ.

4 רָאָה+תֶם = רְאִיתֶם

עָשָׂה+תֶם = עֲשִׂיתֶם, זָכַר+תֶּם = זְכַרְתֶּם,

הָיָה+תֶם = הֱיִיתֶם.

5 בֵּן+■ֵי = בְּנֵי

כָּנָף+■ֵי = כַּנְפֵי .

WORD BEGINNINGS

1 **וְ+אָמַרְתָּ=וְאָמַרְתָּ** וְ+עָשׂוּ=וְעָשׂוּ, וְ+נָתְנוּ=וְנָתְנוּ,

וְ+הָיָה=וְהָיָה, וְ+אַחֲרֵי=וְאַחֲרֵי,

וְ+לֹא=וְלֹא .

2 **לְ+דֹרֹתָם=לְדֹרֹתָם** לְ+צִיצִת=לְצִיצִת, לְ+מַעַן=לְמַעַן.

3 **וּ+רְאִיתֶם=וּרְאִיתֶם** וּ+זְכַרְתֶּם=וּזְכַרְתֶּם.

WORD FAMILIES

1 מִצְוָה, מִצְוֹת, מִצְוֹתָי.

2 הָיָה, וִהְיִיתֶם, לִהְיוֹת.

TEFILLAH PHRASES

1 וַעֲשִׂיתֶם אֹתָם, וְאַחֲרֵי עֵינֵיכֶם, וּרְאִיתֶם אֹתוֹ.

2 אַחֲרֵי לְבַבְכֶם, פְּתִיל תְּכֵלֶת, אֲשֶׁר הוֹצֵאתִי אֶתְכֶם.

3 אֲנִי יְיָ אֱלֹהֵיכֶם, וִהְיִיתֶם קְדֹשִׁים, לִהְיוֹת לָכֶם לֵאלֹהִים.

4 מֵאֶרֶץ מִצְרַיִם, עַל כַּנְפֵי בִגְדֵיהֶם, וַעֲשִׂיתֶם אוֹתָם.

5 וַיֹּאמֶר יְיָ, לְמַעַן תִּזְכְּרוּ, וְאָמַרְתָּ אֲלֵהֶם, כָּל מִצְוֹתָי .

AND GOD SPOKE

This is the third section of the* שְׁמַע יִשְׂרָאֵל*. This section of the* שְׁמַע יִשְׂרָאֵל *contains the comandment of the* צִיצִית*. There is also a reference to the Exodus from Egypt.

1. And Adonai spoke to Moses, saying:	1 וַיֹּאמֶר יְיָ אֶל משֶׁה לֵּאמֹר:
2. "Speak to the children of Israel,	2 דַּבֵּר אֶל בְּנֵי יִשְׂרָאֵל,
3. And say to them,	3 וְאָמַרְתָּ אֲלֵהֶם,
4. And tell them to put tzitzit,	4 וְעָשׂוּ לָהֶם צִיצִת,
5. On the corners of their clothing, for all their generations.	5 עַל כַּנְפֵי בִגְדֵיהֶם לְדֹרֹתָם.
6. And they shall place on the corner tzitzit	6 וְנָתְנוּ עַל צִיצִת הַכָּנָף
7. A blue thread.	7 פְּתִיל תְּכֵלֶת.
8. And it shall be for you tzitzit,	8 וְהָיָה לָכֶם לְצִיצִת,
9. And you shall see it	9 וּרְאִיתֶם אֹתוֹ
10. And you will remember all of Adonai's Mitzvot,	10 וּזְכַרְתֶּם אֶת כָּל מִצְוֹת יְיָ,
11. And you shall do them,	11 וַעֲשִׂיתֶם אֹתָם,
12. And you shall not stray	12 וְלֹא תָתוּרוּ
13. After (the desire of) your hearts,	13 אַחֲרֵי לְבַבְכֶם,
14. And after your eyes,	14 וְאַחֲרֵי עֵינֵיכֶם,
15. Which you yearn for.	15 אֲשֶׁר אַתֶּם זֹנִים אַחֲרֵיהֶם.
16. So you shall remember	16 לְמַעַן תִּזְכְּרוּ
17. And do all my Mitzvot,	17 וַעֲשִׂיתֶם אֶת כָּל מִצְוֹתָי,
18. And you shall be holy to your God.	18 וִהְיִיתֶם קְדֹשִׁים לֵאלֹהֵיכֶם.
19. I am Adonai your God,	19 אֲנִי יְיָ אֱלֹהֵיכֶם,
20. Who brought you out	20 אֲשֶׁר הוֹצֵאתִי אֶתְכֶם
21. From the land of Egypt,	21 מֵאֶרֶץ מִצְרַיִם,
22. To be your God.	22 לִהְיוֹת לָכֶם לֵאלֹהִים.
23. I am Adonai your God.	23 אֲנִי יְיָ אֱלֹהֵיכֶם.

PRAYER SHAWL טַלִּית

The תּוֹרָה instructs us to "make fringes on the corners of your garments" (Numbers 15:38). The garment with the fringes is the טַלִּית. The צִיצִת are the fringes which are attached at the four corners. The טַלִּית is the prayer shawl worn by some congregants during the morning prayer on weekdays, Shabbats, and festivals. The טַלִּית has sometimes been called the "badge of holiness." It is a constant reminder of a Jew's responsibilities to God.

Our sages said, "The world is based on three principles: on the Torah, on prayer, and on good deeds." This means that you have three ways to achieve a happier and more ethical Jewish life.

Your mind can reach out and be enriched with Jewish history, Jewish customs,and Jewish books and the Torah.

Your heart can reach out and touch the holiness of God by prayer with כַּוָּנָה*.*

Your hands can become stronger by doing מִצְוֹת *and helping those less fortunate than you.*

Your rabbi and instructors are preparing you to travel on the road of Torah, prayer and מִצְוֹת*. It is your responsibility to learn these principles and commit yourself to them.*

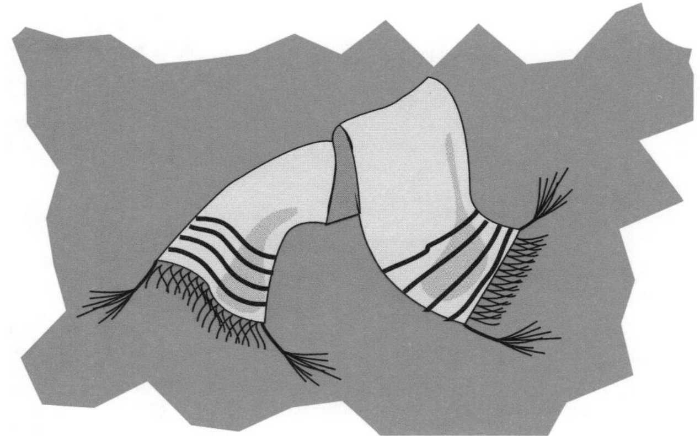

The Biblical commandment on line 7 states that a thread in the צִיצִת should contain a blue cord. The rabbis said that the blue resembles the color of the sky where God lives. In ancient times the dye for the blue cord was extracted from a snail found only in a few seashore areas on the Mediterranean coast. The rabbis stopped using the blue thread because they could not find the special snail.

THE BLUE THREAD פְּתִיל תְּכֵלֶת

The blue thread is said to represent the link between life in the upper world, in the blue sky and the blue waters in the lower world, in the seas, lakes and oceans. The blue skies are filled with a rainbow of flying creatures. While the blue waters are filled with creatures ranging from tiny plankton to electric eels, talking dolphins and spouting whales. All of God's creatures in the blue sky and in the blue seas and on earth are tied together into one complete world.

HALF KADDISH

On these two facing pages you will learn to read some of the words and phrases found in the second part of the חֲצִי קַדִּישׁ.

WORD ENDINGS

בְּחַיֵּי+כוֹן=בְּחַיֵּיכוֹן 1

בְּיוֹמֵי+כוֹן=בְּיוֹמֵיכוֹן .

בְּרָכָא+תָא=בִּרְכָתָא 2

שִׁירָא+תָא=שִׁירָתָא,

נְחָמָא+תָא=נֶחֱמָתָא ,

תֻּשְׁבְּחָא+תָא=תֻּשְׁבְּחָתָא .

רְעוּת+■ֵהּ=רְעוּתֵהּ 3

מַלְכוּת+■ֵהּ=מַלְכוּתֵהּ .

WORD BEGINNINGS

1 יִתְ+גַּדַּל = יִתְגַּדַּל   יִתְ+קַדַּשׁ = יִתְקַדַּשׁ,   יִתְ+בָּרַךְ = יִתְבָּרַךְ,

יִתְ+פָּאַר = יִתְפָּאַר,   יִתְ+רֹמַם = יִתְרֹמַם,

יִתְ+הַלַּל = יִתְהַלַּל .

2 לְ+עָלַם = לְעָלַם   לְ+עֵלָּא = לְעֵלָּא,   לְ+עָלְמֵי = לְעָלְמֵי .

3 וְ+יַמְלִיךְ = וְיַמְלִיךְ   וְ+יִשְׁתַּבַּח = וְיִשְׁתַּבַּח,   וְ+יִתְנַשֵּׂא = וְיִתְנַשֵּׂא,

וְ+יִתְהַדַּר = וְיִתְהַדַּר,   וְ+נֶחֱמָתָא = וְנֶחֱמָתָא,

וְ+יִתְעַלֶּה = וְיִתְעַלֶּה,   וְ+אִמְרוּ = וְאִמְרוּ .

4 וּ+בְחַיֵּי = וּבְחַיֵּי   וּ+בְיוֹמֵיכוֹן = וּבְיוֹמֵיכוֹן .

WORD FAMILIES

1 יִתְקַדַּשׁ,   קֻדְשָׁא.   מְבָרַךְ,   בְּרִיךְ,   בִּרְכָתָא,   יִתְבָּרַךְ.

2 לְעָלַם,   לְעָלְמֵי,   עָלְמַיָּא,   בְּעָלְמָא .

TEFILLAH PHRASES

1 דַּאֲמִירָן בְּעָלְמָא,   יִתְבָּרַךְ וְיִשְׁתַּבַּח,   יִתְגַּדַּל וְיִתְקַדַּשׁ.

2 וְיִתְנַשֵּׂא וְיִתְהַדַּר,   דְכָל-בֵּית יִשְׂרָאֵל,   בְּרִיךְ הוּא,   וְיִתְהַדַּר וְיִתְעַלֶּה.

3 וּבִזְמַן קָרִיב,   כָּל-בִּרְכָתָא,   יְהֵא שְׁמֵהּ רַבָּא מְבָרַךְ,   וְאִמְרוּ אָמֵן.

HALF KADDISH

The חֲצִי קַדִּישׁ is recited during all the prayer services. At the Saturday morning service it is recited twice. The חֲצִי קַדִּישׁ marks the end of the sections of the prayer services.

Reader:

1. Exalted and praised is God's great name,	1 יִתְגַּדַּל וְיִתְקַדַּשׁ שְׁמֵהּ רַבָּא,
2. In the world created according to God's will,	2 בְּעָלְמָא דִּי בְרָא כִרְעוּתֵהּ,
3. And may your rule be established,	3 וְיַמְלִיךְ מַלְכוּתֵהּ,
4. In our life time, and in your day.	4 בְּחַיֵּיכוֹן וּבְיוֹמֵיכוֹן.
5. And in the lifetime of the entire House of Israel	5 וּבְחַיֵּי דְכָל-בֵּית יִשְׂרָאֵל
6. Speedily and in the near future.	6 בַּעֲגָלָא וּבִזְמַן קָרִיב.
7. And let us say amen. Congregation: אָמֵן	7 וְאִמְרוּ אָמֵן.

Congregation and Reader:

8. May God's great name be blessed	8 יְהֵא שְׁמֵהּ רַבָּא מְבָרַךְ
9. For ever and ever.	9 לְעָלַם וּלְעָלְמֵי עָלְמַיָּא.

Reader:

10. Blessed, praised, and exalted	10 יִתְבָּרַךְ וְיִשְׁתַּבַּח וְיִתְפָּאַר
11. Glorified and exalted,	11 וְיִתְרוֹמַם וְיִתְנַשֵּׂא,
12. Uplifted and honored	12 וְיִתְהַדַּר וְיִתְעַלֶּה
13. Praised be the name of the Holy One.	13 וְיִתְהַלַּל שְׁמֵהּ דְּקֻדְשָׁא.

Congregation and Reader:

14. Blessed is God.	14 בְּרִיךְ הוּא.

Reader:

15. Above all blessings and hymns,	15 לְעֵלָּא מִן כָּל-בִּרְכָתָא וְשִׁירָתָא,
16. Praises and consolations,	16 תֻּשְׁבְּחָתָא וְנֶחֱמָתָא,
17. Which we utter in the world,	17 דַּאֲמִירָן בְּעָלְמָא,
18. And let us say amen.	18 וְאִמְרוּ אָמֵן.

Congregation: אָמֵן

KADDISH קַדִּישׁ

The קַדִּישׁ is written in Aramaic, the language spoken by the Jewish people in the ancient Middle East for about a thousand years after the Babylonian captivity. Even the Talmud, which records the discussions of our rabbis, is written in Aramaic.The Hebrew root of קַדִּישׁ is קָדוֹשׁ, which means "holy."

For a young person, death is a very difficult event to think about. Losing a friend, relative, or family member is a very sad experience in your young life. It is like losing a piece of yourself. Reciting the קַדִּישׁ in front of other people can help ease the mourner's mind.

If you have lost someone, try thinking about the good times you had together. Try to remember something the person taught you or a funny thing the departed person did, vacations you shared, achievements, songs, foods, or books that he or she liked.

There are several forms of קַדִּישׁ. The original form was recited as a short prayer at the end of a sermon by a rabbi. Since many of the discussions and sermons were in Aramaic, the closing prayer was in the same language. This קַדִּישׁ is called the קַדִּישׁ דְּרַבָּנָן. Sometime later a different form of the קַדִּישׁ was inserted to mark the end of the sections of the prayer service. This was called the חֲצִי קַדִּישׁ (Half Kaddish).

יאָרצַייט

The observance of the anniversary of a parent's death is called יאָרצַייט. The Yiddish term Yahrzeit is made up of two German words: יאָר, meaning "year," and צַייט, meaning "time." This custom originated in Germany during the fifteenth century.

יאָרצַייט is observed on the date of the parent's death. It is customary to light a יאָרצַייט candle or lamp on the evening of the ceremony. The יאָרצַייט lamp should remain burning until the sunset of the next day.During the יאָרצַייט, the individual recites the mourner's קַדִּישׁ יָתוֹם at every service.

MOURNER'S KADDISH קַדִּישׁ יָתוֹם

For parents who have passed away, there is a קַדִּישׁ יָתוֹם (Mourner's Kaddish).

The קַדִּישׁ יָתוֹם is recited by the Traditional and Conservative Jews at every service for eleven months after a death in the family.

HOW TO RECITE THE
עֲמִידָה

The עֲמִידָה is recited in a special way.

1. You stand with feet together facing the Aron Kodesh. You face the Ark or East, if there is no Ark, because the city of Jerusalem is in the East.

2. You recite the עֲמִידָה silently.

3. When you finish the עֲמִידָה, you take three small steps backward and bow. The word עֲמִידָה means standing. Each of the three daily services שַׁחֲרִית, מִנְחָה and מַעֲרִיב is highlighted by the silent עֲמִידָה. During this prayer the worshipper remains standing and silently recites the עֲמִידָה prayers.

AMIDAH עֲמִידָה

The Shabbat עֲמִידָה differs from the weekday עֲמִידָה. On Shabbat the thirteen middle benedictions drop out and are replaced by a single benediction called קְדוּשַׁת הַיּוֹם. The Talmud says, "On Shabbat one recites seven including קְדוּשַׁת הַיּוֹם in the middle."

On Shabbat the עֲמִידָה consists of only seven blessings – the seven are divided into three catagories:

1. Praises: the first three blessings are exactly the same as the blessings in the daily עֲמִידָה
2. Holiness of the Day: the middle 13 blessings of the daily עֲמִידָה are omitted. In their place is the fourth blessing for Shabbat.

This blessing contains a reminder of the Ten Commandments of Mt. Sinai and how God gave us the Shabbat, the day of rest. We also ask God to help us observe the Mitzvot.

3. Thanksgiving: the last three blessings are the same as in the daily עֲמִידָה.

The עֲמִידָה has been arranged in the form of a ladder which connects heaven to earth. This ladder is similar to the ladder of the patriarch Jacob.

1. The salutation consists of the first three prayers which praise God.

2. Blessings and requests. The next 13 blessings, which make a total of 16.

3. Taking leave – the last 3 are expressions of gratitude for a total of 19.

Another name for the עֲמִידָה is שְׁמוֹנֶה עֶשְׂרֵה. The words mean 18. It is called שְׁמוֹנֶה עֶשְׂרֵה because the prayer section originally contained 18 blessings. Sometime later a 19th blessing was added, but the name שְׁמוֹנֶה עֶשְׂרֵה was retained, as were many of the prayers arranged by the men of the Great Assembly during the days of the Second Temple. During the morning שַׁחֲרִית and afternoon מִנְחָה service, the עֲמִידָה is repeated by the leader for the sake of those who have difficulty reading it themselves. On special occasions such as Hanukah, Purim, Fast Days, or Rosh Hodesh (new moon) other prayers are added to the שְׁמוֹנֶה עֶשְׂרֵה.

ANCESTORS

***On these two facing pages you will learn to read some of the words and phrases found in the prayer* אָבוֹת.**

WORD ENDINGS

1	אֱלֹהִים+■ֵינוּ=אֱלֹהֵינוּ	אָבוֹת+■ֵינוּ=אֲבוֹתֵינוּ.
2	חֶסֶד+■ִים=חֲסָדִים	טוֹב+■ִים=טוֹבִים.
3	אֱלֹהִים+■ֵי=אֱלֹהֵי	חֲסָדִים+■ֵי=חַסְדֵי, בָּנִים+■ֵי=בְּנֵי.

WORD BEGINNINGS

1 וְ+הַנּוֹרָא=וְהַנּוֹרָא   וְ+זוֹכֵר=וְזוֹכֵר,   וְ+קוֹנֵה=וְקוֹנֵה.

2 הָ+אֵל=הָאֵל   הַ+גָּדוֹל=הַגָּדוֹל,   הַ+גִּבּוֹר=הַגִּבּוֹר.

3 וּ+מֵבִיא=וּמֵבִיא   וּ+מוֹשִׁיעַ=וּמוֹשִׁיעַ.

WORD FAMILIES

1 הָאֵל   אֱלֹהֵי,   אֱלֹהֵינוּ.   בְּנֵיהֶם,   בְּנֵי.

2 אָבוֹת,   אֲבוֹתֵינוּ.   חֲסָדִים,   חַסְדֵי.

TEFILLAH PHRASES

1 הָאֵל הַגָּדוֹל,   מָגֵן אַבְרָהָם,   חֲסָדִים טוֹבִים,   אֱלֹהֵי אַבְרָהָם.

2 הַגִּבּוֹר וְהַנּוֹרָא,   וֵאלֹהֵי יַעֲקֹב,   וְקוֹנֵה הַכֹּל,   וּמוֹשִׁיעַ וּמָגֵן.

3 אֵל עֶלְיוֹן,   אֱלֹהֵי יִצְחָק,   וּמֵבִיא גוֹאֵל,   בָּרוּךְ אַתָּה יְיָ.

4 לְמַעַן שְׁמוֹ,   וֵאלֹהֵי אֲבוֹתֵינוּ,   חַסְדֵי אָבוֹת,   לִבְנֵי בְנֵיהֶם.

ANCESTORS

The* אָבוֹת *prayer is the first blessing of the* עֲמִידָה*.

אֲדֹנָי, שְׂפָתַי תִּפְתָּח וּפִי יַגִּיד תְּהִלָּתֶךָ

1. Blessed are you, Adonai	1 בָּרוּךְ אַתָּה יְיָ,
2. Our God and God of our ancestors	2 אֱלֹהֵינוּ וֵאלֹהֵי אֲבוֹתֵינוּ,
3. The God of Abraham, the God of Isaac,	3* אֱלֹהֵי אַבְרָהָם אֱלֹהֵי יִצְחָק
4. And the God of Jacob.	4 וֵאלֹהֵי יַעֲקֹב,
5. The great, mighty, and awesome God,	5 הָאֵל הַגָּדוֹל הַגִּבּוֹר וְהַנּוֹרָא,
6. God on high.	6 אֵל עֶלְיוֹן,
7. You bestow great kindness	7 גּוֹמֵל חֲסָדִים טוֹבִים
8. And create everything	8 וְקוֹנֵה הַכֹּל,
9. And remember the good deeds of our ancestors,	9 וְזוֹכֵר חַסְדֵי אָבוֹת*
10. Who will bring a redeemer	10 וּמֵבִיא גוֹאֵל
11. To their children's children.	11 לִבְנֵי בְנֵיהֶם
12. Because of God's Name with love,	12 לְמַעַן שְׁמוֹ* בְּאַהֲבָה.
13. Ruler, Helper, Deliverer, and Shield	13 מֶלֶךְ עוֹזֵר וּמוֹשִׁיעַ וּמָגֵן.
14. Blessed are You, Adonai,	14 בָּרוּךְ אַתָּה יְיָ,
15. Shield of Abraham.	15 מָגֵן אַבְרָהָם. אָמֵן

*The ancestors of the tribes of Israel were the matriarchs and patriarchs. Some Conservative prayerbooks have added the names of the matriarchs to lines 3 and 4.
In those prayerbooks line 3 reads: אֱלֹהֵי אַבְרָהָם וְשָׂרָה אֱלֹהֵי יִצְחָק וְרִבְקָה The God of Abraham and Sarah, God of Isaac and Rebecca.
Line 4 reads: וֵאלֹהֵי יַעֲקֹב וְלֵאָה וְרָחֵל and the God of Jacob and Leah and Rachel.
Line 15 reads: מָגֵן אַבְרָהָם וְשָׂרָה Shield of Abraham and Sarah.
In the Reform prayerbook line 2 reads אֱלֹהֵינוּ וֵאלֹהֵי אֲבוֹתֵינוּ וְאִמּוֹתֵנוּ.
The words אֱלֹהֵי שָׂרָה, אֱלֹהֵי רִבְקָה, אֱלֹהֵי לֵאָה, וֵאלֹהֵי רָחֵל The God of Sarah, the God of Rebecca, the God of Leah, and the God of Rachel. have been added after line 4.
Line 9 reads וְזוֹכֵר חַסְדֵי אָבוֹת וְאִמָּהוֹת And remember the good deeds of our ancestors.
Line 15 reads מָגֵן אַבְרָהָם וְעֶזְרַת שָׂרָה Shield of Abraham and Sarah's help.

ANCESTORS אָבוֹת

This is the first blessing of every עֲמִידָה, daily, Sabbath or holidays. It is called אָבוֹת, meaning ancestors. It is called ancestors because it contains the names of the three patriarchs of Israel, Abraham, Isaac and Jacob. These three and their wives, Sarah, Rebecca, Leah and Rachel were the cornerstones of the Jewish people. The four wives are known as the matriarchs of Israel. Their names are added to the עֲמִידָה by some Jews to day

מַעֲרִיב מִנְחָה ,שַׁחֲרִית

The Talmud traces the origin of the three daily services שַׁחֲרִית morning, מִנְחָה afternoon and מַעֲרִיב evening to Abraham, Isaac and Jacob.

1. Abraham prayed in the morning.
2. Isaac prayed in the afternoon.
3. Jacob prayed at night.

Think how many autombile accidents there would be if there were no speed limits and traffic lights. Now, just imagine what your life would be like if there was no God, no Commandments, and everything was permitted. The good news is that God has given you an inborn sense of right and wrong. You know and feel it when someone or something is just plain wrong or not fair. That sense is God's presence in you. When you choose the path of the patriarchs and matriarchs of Israel, you are on the path of goodness, truthfulness, and justice,

FAMILY TREE OF THE PATRIARCHS AND MATRIARCHS

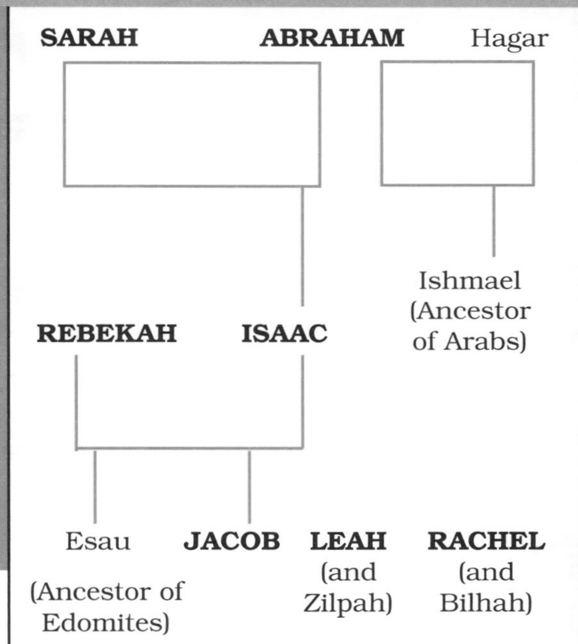

HOW TO RECITE אָבוֹת

You bend your knees and bow when reciting the בָּרוּךְ אַתָּה on line 1. The Hebrew word יְיָ should be said while standing upright.

HOLINESS

On these two facing pages you will learn to read some of the words and phrases that are found in the קְדוּשָׁה prayer for the Musaf service. There are several variations of the קְדוּשָׁה.

WORD ENDINGS

מַקְדִּישׁ + ■ִים = מַקְדִּישִׁים 1

שׁוֹאֵל + ■ִים = שׁוֹאֲלִים,

פַּעַם + ■ִים = פַּעֲמַיִם,

אוֹמֵר + ■ִים = אוֹמְרִים,

מְיַחֵד + ■ִים = מְיַחֲדִים.

מוֹשִׁיעַ + נוּ = מוֹשִׁיעֵנוּ 2

אָב + נוּ = אָבִינוּ, אֱלֹהִים + נוּ = אֱלֹהֵינוּ,

יַשְׁמִיעַ + נוּ = יַשְׁמִיעֵנוּ,

מֶלֶךְ + נוּ = מַלְכֵּנוּ.

כָּבוֹד + וֹ = כְּבוֹדוֹ 3

מָקוֹם + וֹ = מְקוֹמוֹ, שֵׁם + וֹ = שְׁמוֹ,

יֹאמַר + וּ = יֹאמְרוּ.

נַעֲרִיץ + ךָ = נַעֲרִיצְךָ 4

נַקְדִּישׁ + ךָ = נַקְדִּישְׁךָ, שֵׁם + ךָ = שִׁמְךָ,

נָבִיא + ךָ = נְבִיאֶךָ.

WORD BEGINNINGS

1 וְ+קָרָא=וְקָרָא וְ+נַקְדִּישְׁךָ=וְנַקְדִּישְׁךָ, וְ+אָמַר=וְאָמַר, וְ+הוּא=וְהוּא.

2 הַ+מְיַחֲדִים=הַמְיַחֲדִים הַ+מַקְדִּישִׁים=הַמַּקְדִּישִׁים.

3 בְּ+כָל=בְּכָל בְּ+רַחֲמִים=בְּרַחֲמִים, בְּ+אַהֲבָה=בְּאַהֲבָה.

WORD FAMILIES

1 קֹדֶשׁ, קָדוֹשׁ, קָדְשְׁךָ, הַמַּקְדִּישִׁים, וְנַקְדִּישְׁךָ.

2 כְּבוֹדוֹ, כְּבוֹד. לֵאלֹהִים, אֱלֹהַיִךְ, אֱלֹהֵיכֶם.

3 יֹאמֵרוּ, לֵאמֹר, וְאָמַר.

TEFILLAH PHRASES

1 הוּא מַלְכֵּנוּ, מָלֵא עוֹלָם, מְשָׁרְתָיו שׁוֹאֲלִים, לִהְיוֹת לָכֶם.

2 מְקוֹם כְּבוֹדוֹ, יוֹם תָּמִיד, עַם הַמְיַחֲדִים, אֲנִי יְיָ, יְיָ אֱלֹהֵינוּ.

3 יְיָ אֶחָד, זֶה לָזֶה, בָּרוּךְ יֹאמֵרוּ, שְׁמַע אוֹמְרִים.

4 כְּסוֹד שִׂיחַ, עֶרֶב וָבֹקֶר, פַּעֲמַיִם בְּאַהֲבָה.

HOLINESS

After the second blessing of the Amidah, the congregation stands to join the cantor in reciting the קְדוּשָׁה. The קְדוּשָׁה—holiness prayer is a preface to the third blessing in the עֲמִידָה. There are several versions of the קְדוּשָׁה.

Reader and Congregation:

1. We will revere and declare You holy, — 1 נַעֲרִיצְךָ וְנַקְדִּישְׁךָ,

2. According to the mystic speech of the holy angels — 2 כְּסוֹד שִׂיחַ שַׂרְפֵי קֹדֶשׁ

3. Who declare the holiness of Your name — 3 הַמַּקְדִּישִׁים שִׁמְךָ בַּקֹּדֶשׁ

4. As written by the hands of your prophet. — 4 כַּכָּתוּב עַל יַד נְבִיאֶךָ.

5. Each (heavenly body) called to each other and said: — 5 וְקָרָא זֶה אֶל זֶה וְאָמַר.

Congregation and Reader:

6. Adonai of Hosts is Holy, Holy, Holy — 6 קָדוֹשׁ קָדוֹשׁ קָדוֹשׁ יְיָ צְבָאוֹת

7. All the universe is filled with God's glory. — 7 מְלֹא כָל הָאָרֶץ כְּבוֹדוֹ*.

Reader

8. God's glory fills the universe — 8 כְּבוֹדוֹ* מָלֵא עוֹלָם

9. The ministering angels ask each other — 9 מְשָׁרְתָיו* שׁוֹאֲלִים זֶה לָזֶה

10. Where is the source of God's glory? — 10 אַיֵּה מְקוֹם כְּבוֹדוֹ?

11. Those facing them say, "Blessed." — 11 לְעֻמָּתָם בָּרוּךְ יֹאמֵרוּ.

Congregation and Reader:

12. Blessed is the glory of Adonai — 12 בָּרוּךְ כְּבוֹד יְיָ

Reader

13. From the Source. — 13 מִמְּקוֹמוֹ.*

14. Adonai will turn in mercy and be gracious — 14 הוּא יִפֶן בְּרַחֲמִים וְיָחוֹן

15. To the people who proclaim the oneness of the Name — 15 עַם הַמְיַחֲדִים שְׁמוֹ*

16. Evening and morning, always every day — 16 עֶרֶב וָבֹקֶר בְּכָל יוֹם תָּמִיד

17. Twice a day with love they recite Shma. — 17 פַּעֲמַיִם בְּאַהֲבָה שְׁמַע אוֹמְרִים.

Congregation and Reader:

18. Hear O Israel	18 שְׁמַע יִשְׂרָאֵל
19. Adonai is our God, Adonai is One.	19 יְיָ אֱלֹהֵינוּ יְיָ אֶחָד.

Reader

20. Adonai is our God,	20 הוּא* אֱלֹהֵינוּ,
21. Adonai is our Ancestor,	21 הוּא אָבִינוּ,
22. Adonai is our Ruler,	22 הוּא מַלְכֵּנוּ,
23. Adonai is our Deliverer,	23 הוּא מוֹשִׁיעֵנוּ,
24. Adonai will mercifully listen to us	24 וְהוּא יַשְׁמִיעֵנוּ בְּרַחֲמָיו*
25. A second time, before the eyes of all living things	25 שֵׁנִית לְעֵינֵי כָּל חָי
26. To be your God.	26 לִהְיוֹת לָכֶם לֵאלֹהִים.

Congregation and Reader:

27. I am Adonai your God.	27 אֲנִי יְיָ אֱלֹהֵיכֶם.

Reader

28. In Your holy words, it is written, saying,	28 וּבְדִבְרֵי קָדְשְׁךָ כָּתוּב לֵאמֹר,

Congregation and Reader:

26. Adonai will rule forever,	29 יִמְלֹךְ יְיָ לְעוֹלָם,
27. Your God, O, Zion,	30 אֱלֹהַיִךְ צִיּוֹן,
28. For generation after generation, Halleluyah.	31 לְדֹר וָדֹר הַלְלוּיָהּ.

HOW TO RECITE THE קְדוּשָׁה

1. The קְדוּשָׁה is only recited with a minyan. 2. It is recited while standing with feet together. 3. At the recitation of the word קָדוֹשׁ קָדוֹשׁ קָדוֹשׁ, on line 6, you raise yourself on your toes three times. This custom comes from the phrase in the Book of Isaiah, "And with two wings they fluttered about."

During the fifth century, the Persians persecuted the Jews and forbade them to recite the שְׁמַע. So, the Rabbis slipped parts of the שְׁמַע into the קְדוּשָׁה. After the Persians stopped their persecutions, the rabbis retained the phraseology.

שְׂרָפִים

According to the Prophet Isaiah, the שְׂרָפִים are angels who surround the throne of God. They look like earthly beings and have three pairs of wings. The שְׂרָפִים patrol around the throne of God and continually proclaim.

קָדוֹשׁ קָדוֹשׁ קָדוֹשׁ יְיָ צְבָאוֹת
מְלֹא כָל הָאָרֶץ כְּבוֹדוֹ.

כַּוָּנָה

Quiet time spent with your thoughts gives you a chance to think about who and what you are and where you want to go in life. It is good to spend a few quiet moments wandering through your memory and thinking about the good things and the problems in your life. Take a moment, read a prayer and think, about how you can apply it to your life. Take a moment and search your heart for your most cherished dream. Are you willing to raise your effort to run, work, sweat, and study to achieve your personal goals? When you are willing, confidence will come and the way will unfold. If you are willing, God has given you a birth gift to make your dream come true

[24] וְהוּא יַשְׁמִיעֵנוּ בְּרַחֲמָיו And God will mercifully listen to you.

The Bible commentator Jonathan ben Uzziel interprets the words קָדוֹשׁ קָדוֹשׁ קָדוֹשׁ to mean that God is holy up in the heavens down on earth and in the fourth dimension of time.

Another commentator called Malbim added to the commentary by explaining;

1. God is different from earth because God is not formed out of any matter.
2. God is different from the heavens because God has no form.
3. God is different from time because God has no beginning, and no end. God is eternal.

SACRED TORAH OBJECTS

In your synagogue you find ceremonial objects. They are symbols of your faith. To know about them is to have more respect for them, for they are the bond connecting you with your faith, your history and your people.

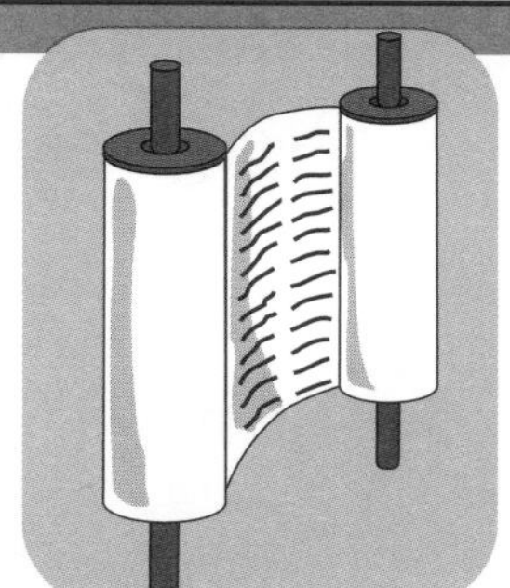

תּוֹרָה

תּוֹרָה which means "teaching" or "law" is a scroll made of especially prepared parchment, and is the basis of the Jewish way of life. The Five Books of Moses that it contains may be written only by hand and without punctuation or vowel points.

אֲרוֹן קֹדֶשׁ

We keep the scrolls of the Torah in the אֲרוֹן קֹדֶשׁ or "holy ark." This chest or closet is named after the Aron Ha-Brit, the Ark of the Covenant, which held the Ten Commandments when our ancestors crossed the desert. The אֲרוֹן קֹדֶשׁ is placed against the wall of the synagogue facing east or toward Jerusalem.

פָּרֹכֶת

Just as the Children of Israel hung a curtain before the Ark of the Covenant, so do we follow their ancient example in our synagogues today. The פָּרֹכֶת, or curtain, is made of satin, velvet or other fine material and is richly embroidered,usually with the Ten Commandments.

כֶּתֶר תּוֹרָה

Over the upper ends of the עֲצֵי חַיִּם we place the כֶּתֶר תּוֹרָה, the "crown of the Torah." It is usually made of silver and adorned with little bells, and is one of the scroll's chief ornaments.

עֲצֵי חַיִּים

The wooden rollers (the עֲצֵי חַיִּים or "trees of life") on which the scrolls of the Torah are wound are made of hard wood. The Torah, too, is called the עֵץ חַיִּים, the "tree of life".

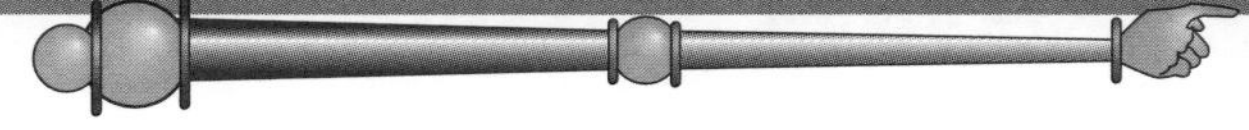

יָד

The pointer of silver or olive wood which is used to guide the reading of the Torah is called the יָד, or "hand". Shaped like a staff, its end is narrow and in the form of a closed fist with the forefinger outstretched.

חוֹשֶׁן

When the Torah is taken out of the Ark, we see its beautiful breastplate suspended by a chain from the top of the rollers. In the center of the breastplate there is frequently a tiny Ark whose doors are in the form of the two tablets of the Law. The lower part of the breastplate has a place where the names of one of the Jewish festivals are displayed on the holiday or sabbath on which the scroll is used.

TODAY'S HOLINESS

On these two facing pages you will learn to read some of the words and phrases found in the קְדוּשַׁת הַיּוֹם.

WORD ENDINGS

1 יָד+וֹ=יָדוֹ

חֵלֶק+וֹ=חֶלְקוֹ, רֹאשׁ+וֹ=רֹאשׁוֹ,

עָמֹד+וֹ=עָמְדוֹ.

2 קָרָא+תָ=קָרָאתָ

נָתַן+תָּ=נָתַתָּ.

3 לִפְנֵי+ךָ=לְפָנֶיךָ

תּוֹרָה+ךָ=תּוֹרָתֶךָ.

4 שְׁנַיִם+■ֵי-שְׁנֵי

בָּנִים+■ֵי-בְּנֵי, לְפָנִים+■ֵי=לִפְנֵי.

WORD BEGINNINGS

1 הָ+אֶרֶץ=הָאָרֶץ הַ+שָּׁמַיִם=הַשָּׁמַיִם, הַ+שְּׁבִיעִי=הַשְּׁבִיעִי,
הַ+שַּׁבָּת=הַשַּׁבָּת.

2 בְּ+יָדוֹ=בְּיָדוֹ בְּ+עָמְדוֹ=בְּעָמְדוֹ, בְּ+מַתְּנַת=בְּמַתְּנַת
בְּ+תוֹרָתֶךָ=בְּתוֹרָתֶךָ.

3 וְ+כָתוּב=וְכָתוּב וְ+אֶת=וְאֶת, וְ+כֵן=וְכֵן,.
וְ+שָׁמְרוּ=וְשָׁמְרוּ.

4 וּ+שְׁנֵי=וּשְׁנֵי וּ+בְיוֹם=וּבְיוֹם.

WORD FAMILIES

1 הַשַּׁבָּת, שָׁבַת. בֵּינִי, וּבֵין. וְשָׁמְרוּ, שְׁמִירַת.

TEFILLAH PHRASES

1 יִשְׂמַח מֹשֶׁה, שֵׁשֶׁת יָמִים, קָרָאתָ לוֹ, בְּרִית עוֹלָם.

2 עֶבֶד נֶאֱמָן, שְׁמִירַת שַׁבָּת, הַר-סִינַי, בְּעָמְדוֹ לְפָנֶיךָ.

3 כְּלִיל תִּפְאֶרֶת, וְכָתוּב בְּתוֹרָתֶךָ, אֶת-הַשָּׁמַיִם, בְּנֵי יִשְׂרָאֵל.

TODAY'S HOLINESS

This is the fourth and middle blessing of the Shabbat Amidah. It thanks God for giving us the holy Shabbat.

יִשְׂמַח מֹשֶׁה

1. Moses was pleased with God's gift.	1 יִשְׂמַח מֹשֶׁה, בְּמַתְּנַת חֶלְקוֹ,
2. For You called him a faithful servant,	2 כִּי עֶבֶד נֶאֱמָן קָרָאתָ לוֹ
3. You placed a glorious crown upon his head,	3 כְּלִיל תִּפְאֶרֶת בְּרֹאשׁוֹ נָתַתָּ,
4. When he stood before You on Mount Sinai.	4 בְּעָמְדוֹ לְפָנֶיךָ עַל הַר-סִינָי.
5. In his hand he brought down two stone tablets	5 וּשְׁנֵי לוּחוֹת אֲבָנִים הוֹרִיד בְּיָדוֹ.
6. On which was written	6 וְכָתוּב בָּהֶם
7. The command to observe Shabbat,	7 שְׁמִירַת שַׁבָּת.
8. And so it is written in Your Torah.	8 וְכֵן כָּתוּב בְּתוֹרָתֶךָ:

וְשָׁמְרוּ בְנֵי יִשְׂרָאֵל

9. And the Children of Israel shall observe Shabbat	9 וְשָׁמְרוּ בְנֵי יִשְׂרָאֵל אֶת הַשַּׁבָּת,
10. To keep the Sabbath,	10 לַעֲשׂוֹת אֶת הַשַּׁבָּת
11. For generations as an everlasting covenant,	11 לְדֹרֹתָם בְּרִית עוֹלָם.
12. Between Me and the Children of Israel,	12 בֵּינִי וּבֵין בְּנֵי יִשְׂרָאֵל
13. It is an eternal sign,	13 אוֹת הִיא לְעֹלָם,
14. Because in six days, Adonai created	14 כִּי שֵׁשֶׁת יָמִים עָשָׂה יְיָ
15. The heavens and the earth,	15 אֶת-הַשָּׁמַיִם וְאֶת-הָאָרֶץ,
16. And on the seventh day God stopped and rested.	16 וּבַיּוֹם הַשְּׁבִיעִי שָׁבַת וַיִּנָּפַשׁ.

עֲשֶׂרֶת הַדִּבְּרוֹת

The Ten Commandments are divided into two groups. There are 6 negative ones and 4 positive ones.

The Midrash tells us that before giving the Torah to the Israelites, God offered it to various other nations of the world.
"Will you accept and obey My Torah?" God asked the first nation.
"What does it say?" they asked. "It says "You shall not kill," answered God.
"We cannot accept and obey the Torah," answered the first nation.
"Throughout our history we have lived by the sword".
Then God asked the second nation, "Will you accept and obey My Torah?"
"What does it say?" they asked.
"It says you shall not steal," answered God.
"We cannot accept and obey the Torah," answered the second nation.
"We live by robbing and kidnapping."
God asked all the nations of the world. But none would promise to accept and obey the Torah. Then God asked Israel. The Israelites did not ask what was in the Torah. They did not hesitate. They answered, "All that God has spoken we will do and we will obey."

The Midrash says that when God gave the עֲשֶׂרֶת הַדִּבְּרוֹת to Israel the whole world was quiet. No birds sang or flew. No lion roared, no angels flew, the seas were calm and no creature spoke, and God said "I am Adonai your God."
The divine voice spoke in all languages, so that everyone in the world could understand the Commandments.

Seven weeks after leaving Egypt, the Israelites camped at the foot of Mount Sinai. Then, the Bible tells us, Moses climbed to the top of the mountain and stayed there for forty days and forty nights. There God gave him the Torah and the Ten Commandments.
God also informed Moses that "if they (Israel) will keep My Commandments, they will be a holy nation." Moses informed the Israelites, and without a moment's hesitation they answered. "We will obey and listen"—נַעֲשֶׂה וְנִשְׁמָע. The Commandments are an important part of your Jewish tradition. For 3,000 years you and your ancestors have been obeying God's laws. Each generation has repeated the same words, נַעֲשֶׂה וְנִשְׁמָע "We will obey and listen." Now it is your turn to become a link in the chain of Jewish tradition. It is time for you to repeat the ancient words נַעֲשֶׂה וְנִשְׁמָע.

TORAH BLESSINGS

On these two facing pages you will learn some of the words and phrases found in בִּרְכוֹת הַתּוֹרָה.

WORD ENDINGS

1 בָּרֵךְ+וּ=בָּרְכוּ — יָפוּץ+וּ=יָפֻצוּ, יָנוּס+וּ=יָנֻסוּ.

2 תּוֹרָה+וֹ=תּוֹרָתוֹ — עַם+וֹ=עַמּוֹ, קְדוּשָּׁה+וֹ=קְדֻשָּׁתוֹ.

3 פָּנִים+■ֶיךָ=פָּנֶיךָ — מְשַׂנְאִים+■ֶיךָ=מְשַׂנְאֶיךָ,

אֹיְבִים+■ֶיךָ=אֹיְבֶיךָ.

WORD BEGINNINGS

1 הַ+מְבֹרָךְ=הַמְבֹרָךְ

הַ+עוֹלָם=הָעוֹלָם, הַ+עַמִּים-הָעַמִּים,
הַ+אָרֹן=הָאָרֹן, הַ+תּוֹרָה=הַתּוֹרָה,
הַ+מֶלֶךְ-מֶּלֶךְ.

2 וְ+נָתַן=וְנָתַן

וְ+חַיֵּי=וְחַיֵּי, וְ+יָפֻצוּ=וְיָפֻצוּ, וְ+יָנֻסוּ=וְיָנֻסוּ.

3 וַ+יְהִי=וַיְהִי

וַ+יֹּאמֶר=וַיֹּאמֶר.

4 מִן+פָּנֶיךָ=מִפָּנֶיךָ

מִן+צִיּוֹן=מִצִּיּוֹן, מִן+יְרוּשָׁלָיִם=מִירוּשָׁלָיִם.

5 בְּ+נְסֹעַ=בִּנְסֹעַ

בְּ+קְדֻשָּׁתוֹ=בִּקְדֻשָּׁתוֹ.

WORD FAMILIES

1 תּוֹרָה, הַתּוֹרָה, תּוֹרַת, תּוֹרָתוֹ. בָּרוּךְ, בָּרְכוּ, הַמְבֹרָךְ.

2 נָתַן, וְנָתַן, שֶׁנָּתַן, נוֹתֵן. עַם, עַמּוֹ, עַמִּים.

TEFILLAH PHRASES

1 לְעוֹלָם וָעֶד, בָּרְכוּ אֶת יְיָ, וַיֹּאמֶר מֹשֶׁה, וּדְבַר-יְיָ.

2 קוּמָה יְיָ, נוֹתֵן הַתּוֹרָה, תּוֹרַת אֱמֶת, וְנָתַן לָנוּ.

3 מִכָּל הָעַמִּים, כִּי מִצִּיּוֹן, אֲשֶׁר בָּחַר בָּנוּ, נָטַע בְּתוֹכֵנוּ.

4 תֵּצֵא תוֹרָה, לְעַמּוֹ יִשְׂרָאֵל, בָּרוּךְ יְיָ הַמְבֹרָךְ.

TORAH BLESSINGS

The ark is opened and the cantor and the congregation sing
וַיְהִי בִּנְסֹעַ הָאָרֹן.

1. And when the Ark went forward Moses said,	1 וַיְהִי בִּנְסֹעַ הָאָרֹן וַיֹּאמֶר מֹשֶׁה,
2. "Rise up, Adonai, and may Your enemies scatter,	2 קוּמָה יהוה וְיָפֻצוּ אֹיְבֶיךָ,
3. And your enemies shall flee before You."	3 וְיָנֻסוּ מְשַׂנְאֶיךָ מִפָּנֶיךָ.
4. For out of Zion the Torah will go forth,	4 כִּי מִצִּיּוֹן תֵּצֵא תוֹרָה,
5. And the Word of Adonai from Jerusalem,	5 וּדְבַר-יהוה מִירוּשָׁלָיִם,
6. Blessed is the One who gave the Torah	6 בָּרוּךְ שֶׁנָּתַן תּוֹרָה
7. In holiness to the people of Israel.	7 לְעַמּוֹ יִשְׂרָאֵל בִּקְדֻשָּׁתוֹ*.

The honoree who is called to the Torah recites:

8. Blessed is Adonai, who is to be blessed.	8 בָּרְכוּ אֶת יְיָ הַמְבֹרָךְ.

The congregation responds:

9. Blessed is Adonai, who is to be blessed forever and ever.	9 בָּרוּךְ יְיָ הַמְבֹרָךְ לְעוֹלָם וָעֶד.

The honoree repeats line 9 and continues until the end of line 14.

10. Blessed are You, Adonai,	10 בָּרוּךְ אַתָּה יְיָ,
11. Our God, Ruler of the world,	11 אֱלֹהֵינוּ מֶלֶךְ הָעוֹלָם,
12. Who has chosen us from all peoples,	12 אֲשֶׁר בָּחַר בָּנוּ מִכָּל הָעַמִּים,
13. And given us Your Torah.	13 וְנָתַן-לָנוּ אֶת תּוֹרָתוֹ*.
14. Blessed are You, Adonai, Giver of the Torah	14 בָּרוּךְ אַתָּה יְיָ, נוֹתֵן הַתּוֹרָה.

After the Torah reader finishes the Torah section, the honoree recites:

15. Blessed are You, Adonai,	15 בָּרוּךְ אַתָּה יְיָ,
16. Our God, Ruler of the world,	16 אֱלֹהֵינוּ מֶלֶךְ הָעוֹלָם,
17. Who has given us the Torah of truth.	17 אֲשֶׁר נָתַן לָנוּ תּוֹרַת אֱמֶת.
18. And planted within us everlasting life.	18 וְחַיֵּי עוֹלָם נָטַע בְּתוֹכֵנוּ,
19. Blessed are You, Adonai, Giver of the Torah.	19 בָּרוּךְ אַתָּה יְיָ, נוֹתֵן הַתּוֹרָה.

Special Torah Readings have been assigned for the festivals, the intermediate days of the festivals and the fastdays. The Torah selections are based upon the significance of the day.

HOW TO RECEIVE AN עֲלִיָּה

1) The congregant who is honored with an עֲלִיָּה comes up to the תּוֹרָה. The reader shows the honoree the place in the Torah where the reading will begin.

2) The honoree touches the Torah with the טַלִּית, then takes hold of the two rollers of the Torah and recites the בָּרְכוּ, (line 8) the call to worship.

3) The congregation responds and says line 9, Then the honoree repeats line 9 and recites the first blessing, lines 10-14. The Torah reader uses a special chant that goes back to ancient times. The musical notes of the chant are called "trop." Tradition tells us that the trop was used during the Torah reading in the days of Ezra and Nehemiah.

4) The second blessing, lines 15-19, is chanted after the תּוֹרָה portion has been read. In it we thank God for giving us the תּוֹרָה. As long as the תּוֹרָה endures, and its teachings are practiced, the Jewish people will also endure.

The תּוֹרָה is divided into fifty-four sections called Sidrot (Parshiyot). There are just enough Sidrot to complete the reading of the entire Torah in one whole year. The cycle of תּוֹרָה readings begins on the Shabbat after Simhat Torah with the reading of the first Sidrah, It ends on Simhat Torah with the reading of the last Sidrah (Parashah),

After the תּוֹרָה reading, a portion from the Prophets is read. This additional reading is called the הַפְטָרָה.

The Torah tells us that when Moses approached the burning bush, the voice of God said, "Remove your sandals, for you are now standing on holy ground."

In ancient days, removing sandals was a sign of respect. Today we have different ways of showing our reverence. The Torah, the prayerbooks, the religious objects, and your rabbi and cantor have made your synagogue into holy ground. Show respect and reverence for your house of worship by dressing neatly and behaving with dignity.

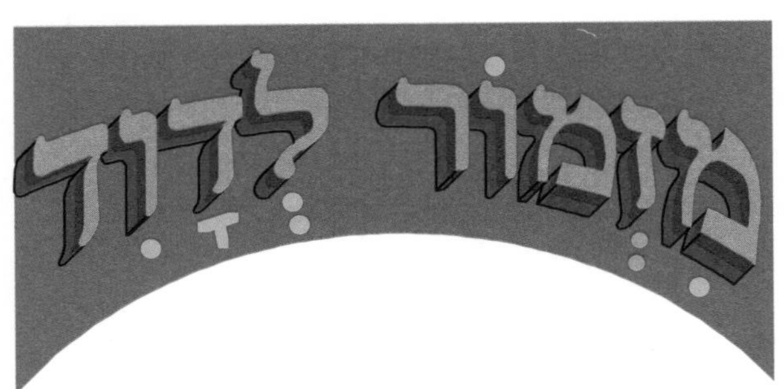

A PSALM OF DAVID

On these two pages you will learn to read some of the words and phrases found in the מִזְמוֹר שִׁיר ***psalm.***

WORD ENDINGS

1 אֵל+■ִים=אֵלִים רַב+■ִים=רַבִּים, אֶרֶז+■ִים=אֲרָזִים,

רְאֵם+■ִים=רְאֵמִים.

2 אֶרֶז+■ֵי=אַרְזֵי בֵּן+■ֵי=בְּנֵי.

3 הֵיכָל+וֹ=הֵיכָלוֹ שֵׁם+וֹ=שְׁמוֹ, עַם+וֹ=עַמּוֹ.

4 לֶהָבָה+וֹת=לַהֲבוֹת אַיָּלָה+וֹת=אַיָּלוֹת, יַעַר+וֹת=יְעָרוֹת.

WORD BEGINNINGS

1 הַ+מַיִם = הַמַּיִם הַ+כָּבוֹד = הַכָּבוֹד, הַ+לְבָנוֹן = הַלְּבָנוֹן.

2 לַ+מַבּוּל = לַמַּבּוּל לַ+יְיָ = לַיְיָ.

3 וַ+יְחֶשֹׂף = וַיֶּחֱשֹׂף וַ+יְשַׁבֵּר = וַיְשַׁבֵּר, וַ+יֵשֶׁב = וַיֵּשֶׁב,
וַ+יַרְקִידֵם = וַיַּרְקִידֵם.

WORD FAMILIES

1 הַמַּיִם, מַיִם. שֹׁבֵר, וַיְשַׁבֵּר. אַרְזֵי, אֲרָזִים. יְיָ, לַיְיָ.
2 בְּהַדְרַת, בֶּהָדָר. יָחִיל, יְחוֹלֵל. יָשָׁב, וַיֵּשֶׁב.

TEFILLAH PHRASES

1 מִזְמוֹר לְדָוִד, בְּנֵי אֵלִים כָּבוֹד וָעֹז, הִשְׁתַּחֲווּ לַיְיָ.
2 קוֹל יְיָ בֶּהָדָר, עַל מַיִם רַבִּים, אַרְזֵי הַלְּבָנוֹן.
3 לַהֲבוֹת אֵשׁ, מִדְבַּר קָדֵשׁ, וַיֵּשֶׁב יְיָ, וַיֶּחֱשֹׂף יְעָרוֹת.
4 יְחוֹלֵל אַיָּלוֹת, בֶּן רְאֵמִים.

A PSALM OF DAVID

The Book of Psalms contains 150 hymns. מִזְמוֹר לְדָוִד is the 29th Psalm. The congregation rises and recites as the Torah is returned to the Ark.

1. A psalm of David	1 מִזְמוֹר לְדָוִד
2. Praise Adonai, children of the mighty,	2 הָבוּ לַייָ בְּנֵי אֵלִים,
3. Praise Adonai's glory and might.	3 הָבוּ לַייָ כָּבוֹד וָעֹז.
4. Praise Adonai's mighty name,	4 הָבוּ לַייָ כְּבוֹד שְׁמוֹ,
5. Bow down to Adonai in splendid holiness,	5 הִשְׁתַּחֲווּ לַייָ בְּהַדְרַת קֹדֶשׁ,
6. Adonai's voice echoes over the waters,	6 קוֹל יְיָ עַל הַמָּיִם,
7. God's might thunders	7 אֵל-הַכָּבוֹד הִרְעִים
8. Adonai is over many waters.	8 יְיָ עַל מַיִם רַבִּים.
9. Adonai's voice is mighty, Adonai's voice is majestic.	9 קוֹל יְיָ בַּכֹּחַ, קוֹל יְיָ בֶּהָדָר.
10. Adonai's voice shatters cedars,	10 קוֹל יְיָ שֹׁבֵר אֲרָזִים,
11. Adonai smashes the cedars of Lebanon,	11 וַיְשַׁבֵּר יְיָ אֶת-אַרְזֵי הַלְּבָנוֹן.
12. God makes them leap like a calf,	12 וַיַּרְקִידֵם כְּמוֹ עֵגֶל,
13. Lebanon and Sirion are like a wild ox.	13 לְבָנוֹן וְשִׂרְיוֹן כְּמוֹ בֶן רְאֵמִים.
14. Adonai's voice shoots flames of fire,	14 קוֹל יְיָ חֹצֵב לַהֲבוֹת אֵשׁ,
15. Adonai's voice causes the wilderness to tremble,	15 קוֹל יְיָ יָחִיל מִדְבָּר,
16. Adonai causes the wilderness of Kadash to quake.	16 יָחִיל יְיָ מִדְבַּר קָדֵשׁ.
17. Adonai's voice causes deer to dance,	17 קוֹל יְיָ יְחוֹלֵל אַיָּלוֹת,
18. And strips the forests bare,	18 וַיֶּחֱשֹׂף יְעָרוֹת,
19. In God's Temple everyone says "Glory."	19 וּבְהֵיכָלוֹ כֻּלּוֹ* אֹמֵר כָּבוֹד.
20. Adonai ruled at the time of the flood,	20 יְיָ לַמַּבּוּל יָשָׁב,
21. Adonai will rule forever.	21 וַיֵּשֶׁב יְיָ מֶלֶךְ לְעוֹלָם.
22. Adonai will give strength to Israel,	22 יְיָ עֹז לְעַמּוֹ* יִתֵּן,
23. Adonai will bless Israel with peace.	23 יְיָ יְבָרֵךְ אֶת עַמּוֹ* בַשָּׁלוֹם.

HYMNS OF PRAISE הַלֵּל

King David's Hymns, the Psalms, are recited in some form at all prayer services. The service of הַלֵּל—Hymns of Praise—consists of six psalms 113-118.
הַלֵּל is recited after the Sabbath Amidah on the holidays of Passover, Shavuot, Shabbat, Hanukah and Rosh Hodesh. Hallel is also recited on the modern holidays of Yom Haatzmaut and Yom Yerushalayim.

Crashing thunderstorms during the winter are frequent in Israel. The ancients saw them as a sign of God's power and anger.
The poet in Psalm 29, pictures a huge noisy thunderstorm. God's voice is the storm that thunders over the waters, shattering mighty cedars and demolishing entire forests. God's voice shoots thunderbolts, causing entire mountains such as Lebanon and Sirion to quake. The storm and the thunder are similar to the giving of the Torah on Mount Sinai. The Torah says, "Now at daybreak on the third day there were peals of thunder on the mountain and lightning flashes, a dense cloud, and a loud trumpet blase, and inside the camp all the people trembled. Then Moses led the people out of the camp to meet God, and they stood at the foot of the mountain. The mountain of Sinai was entirely wrapped in smoke, because Adonai had descended on it in the form of fire. Like smoke from a furnace, the smoke went up, and the whole mountain shook violently."

KING DAVID

As a young man David battled with the Philistines giant Goliath, and killed him with a slingshot. King Saul rewarded David by making him his personal musician and also by giving his daughter, Michal, to him as a wife.
King Saul became jealous of David and wanted to kill him. After many adventures, David became King of Judah when Saul was killed in battle. King David unified the tribes, captured Jerusalem, and enlarged the territory of the kingdom.
David was a great poet and musician. He is credited with writing much of the Book of Psalms. This book consists of 150 hymns, which cover all phases of human life; death, marriage, joy, birth, desolation and triumph. Some Jews regularly recite several psalms each day of the year. Tradition tells us that the Messiah will come from the House of David.

In the future you will be asked, "What was your occupation?" If you reply, "I fed the hungry," then they reply, "This is the gate of God; you who feed the hungry shall enter." (Psalm 118:20). So with giving drink to the thirsty, clothing the naked, with those who look after orphans, and with those, generally, who do deeds of loving-kindness. All these are God's gates, and those who do such deeds shall enter within them.

Midrash Tehillim.

THERE IS NONE LIKE OUR GOD

On these two facing pages you will learn to read some of the words and phrases found in אֵין כֵּאלֹהֵינוּ.

WORD ENDINGS

1 אֱלֹהִים+נוּ=אֱלֹהֵינוּ   אֲדוֹן+נוּ=אֲדוֹנֵינוּ,   אָבוֹת+נוּ=אֲבוֹתֵינוּ,

מֶלֶךְ+נוּ=מַלְכֵּנוּ,   מוֹשִׁיעַ+נוּ=מוֹשִׁיעֵנוּ.

WORD BEGINNINGS

1 כְּ+מַלְכֵּנוּ=כְּמַלְכֵּנוּ   כְּ+מוֹשִׁיעֵנוּ=כְּמוֹשִׁיעֵנוּ.

2 כְ+מַלְכֵּנוּ=כְמַלְכֵּנוּ   כְ+מוֹשִׁיעֵנוּ=כְמוֹשִׁיעֵנוּ.

3 לְ+מַלְכֵּנוּ=לְמַלְכֵּנוּ   לְ+מוֹשִׁיעֵנוּ=לְמוֹשִׁיעֵנוּ.
לְ+פָּנֶיךָ=לְפָנֶיךָ.

WORD FAMILIES

1 מֶלֶךְ, מַלְכֵּנוּ, לְמַלְכֵּנוּ, כְּמַלְכֵּנוּ, כְמַלְכֵּנוּ.

2 מוֹשִׁיעַ, מוֹשִׁיעֵנוּ, לְמוֹשִׁיעֵנוּ, כְּמוֹשִׁיעֵנוּ, כְמוֹשִׁיעֵנוּ.

3 אֱלֹהִים, אֱלֹהֵינוּ, לֵאלֹהֵינוּ, כֵּאלֹהֵינוּ, כֵאלֹהֵינוּ.

4 אֲדוֹנִים, אֲדוֹנֵינוּ, לַאדוֹנֵינוּ, כַּאדוֹנֵינוּ, כַאדוֹנֵינוּ.

TEFILLAH PHRASES

1 אַתָּה הוּא אֱלֹהֵינוּ, קְטֹרֶת הַסַּמִּים, מִי כְמוֹשִׁיעֵנוּ.

2 בָּרוּךְ מוֹשִׁיעֵנוּ, מִי כַאדוֹנֵינוּ, נוֹדֶה לְמַלְכֵּנוּ.

3 אֵין כֵּאלֹהֵינוּ, שֶׁהִקְטִירוּ אֲבוֹתֵינוּ, בָּרוּךְ אֲדוֹנֵינוּ.

4 מִי כֵאלֹהֵינוּ, אַתָּה הוּא מַלְכֵּנוּ, נוֹדֶה לְמוֹשִׁיעֵנוּ.

THERE IS NONE LIKE OUR GOD

The אֵין כֵּאלֹהֵינוּ is recited only on the Shabbat and on Festivals. It is recited at the close of the service.

1. There is none like our God.	1 אֵין כֵּאלֹהֵינוּ.
2. There is none like our Almighty.	2 אֵין כַּאדוֹנֵינוּ.
3. There is none like our Ruler.	3 אֵין כְּמַלְכֵּנוּ.
4. There is none like our Deliverer.	4 אֵין כְּמוֹשִׁיעֵנוּ.
5. Who is like our God?	5 מִי כֵאלֹהֵינוּ?
6. Who is like our Almighty?	6 מִי כַאדוֹנֵינוּ?
7. Who is like our Ruler?	7 מִי כְמַלְכֵּנוּ?
8. Who is like our Deliverer?	8 מִי כְמוֹשִׁיעֵנוּ?
9. Let us thank our God.	9 נוֹדֶה לֵאלֹהֵינוּ.
10. Let us thank our Almighty.	10 נוֹדֶה לַאדוֹנֵינוּ.
11. Let us thank our Ruler.	11 נוֹדֶה לְמַלְכֵּנוּ.
12. Let us thank our Deliverer.	12 נוֹדֶה לְמוֹשִׁיעֵנוּ.
13. Blessed is our God.	13 בָּרוּךְ אֱלֹהֵינוּ.
14. Blessed is our Almighty.	14 בָּרוּךְ אֲדוֹנֵינוּ.
15. Blessed is our Ruler.	15 בָּרוּךְ מַלְכֵּנוּ.
16. Blessed is our Deliverer.	16 בָּרוּךְ מוֹשִׁיעֵנוּ.
17. You are our God!	17 אַתָּה הוּא אֱלֹהֵינוּ!
18. You are our Almighty!	18 אַתָּה הוּא אֲדוֹנֵינוּ!
19. You are our Ruler!	19 אַתָּה הוּא מַלְכֵּנוּ!
20. You are our Deliverer!	20 אַתָּה הוּא מוֹשִׁיעֵנוּ!
21. You are the One,	21 אַתָּה הוּא,
22. Before whom our ancestors burned	22 שֶׁהִקְטִירוּ אֲבוֹתֵינוּ לְפָנֶיךָ
22. The incense offering.	23 אֶת קְטֹרֶת הַסַּמִּים.

אֵין כֵּאלֹהֵינוּ

The first letters of the first three verses, lines 1,5 and 9, make up the word Amen.

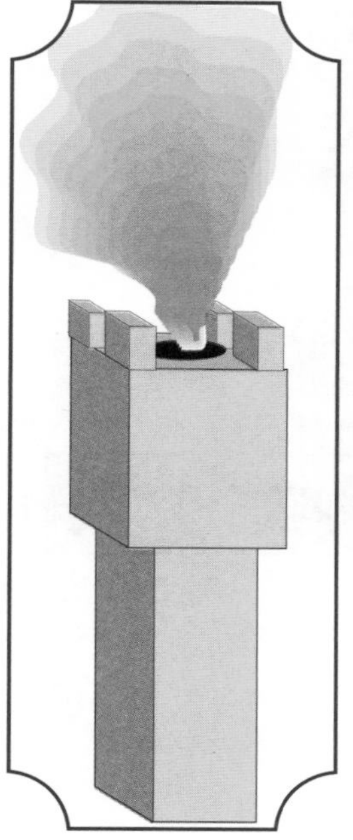

קְטֹרֶת הַסַּמִּים

Incense is made from spices, gums, herbs, and other naturally occurring substances which give off perfume when burned. Sacrifices in the ancient temple were always accompanied by the burning of incense. The Hebrews believed that the sweet-smelling spices made the sacrifices and prayers of the priests more acceptable to God. Incense offerings were brought twice a day, corresponding to the daily morning and afternoon services. On Yom Kippur, the High Priest himself was required to bring an incense offering into the Holy of Holies.

SERVICE OF THE HEART

When the Second Temple was destroyed by the Romans in 70 B.C.E., the temple service was replaced by the synagogue service. Unlike the temple, Priests, Levites and sacrifices were unimportant for the religious mission of the synagogue service. Now, the emphasis was on the people and their prayers as a means of communications with the Almighty. The synagogue now became a portable temple which could be transported wherever Jews decided to live or were forced to settle. New prayers and ceremonies were introduced and the temple sevice and pageantry was replace by the "service of the heart."Our sages taught that the essence of the Torah was to love Adonai with all your heart and with all your soul. They felt that without heartfelt deeds to match them, prayers were just formalized words. As they are spoken, they need to be alive and true. When prayers are true and penetrating they forge a permanent bond with the Almighty. Prayer is the "service of the heart." Put your heart into your words and deeds.

The better you can read the Hebrew prayers, the more you will feel in rhythm with the ideas and spirit of the words. Enter the synagogue, clear your mind of any outside thoughts. Forget about music practice, tennis games, homework, and the upcoming test. Concentrate on the prayer, and sing with feeling and emotion.
אֵין כֵּאלֹהֵינוּ *There is none like our God.*
Get into sync with the rhythm and the music. Once you enter into the emotion of the prayer, it will lift your spirits, and God's presence will move through you.
With all your heart say
"Let us thank our God. נוֹדֶה לֵאלֹהֵינוּ*"*

God has many names. Four of them are used in אֵין כֵּאלֹהֵינוּ:

1. אלֹהֵינוּ Our God
2. אֲדוֹנֵינוּ Our Adonai
3. מוֹשִׁיעֵנוּ Our Deliverer
4. מַלְכֵּנוּ Our Ruler

Jews look upon God as their friend, protector, and ruler, to whom they can turn for hope and inspiration.

IT IS FOR US TO PRAISE

On these two facing pages you will learn someof the words and phrases found in עָלֵינוּ לְשַׁבֵּחַ.

WORD ENDINGS

1 שָׁם+נוּ = שָׁמָנוּ

חֵלֶק+נוּ = חֶלְקֵנוּ, מֶלֶךְ+נוּ = מַלְכֵּנוּ,
אֱלֹהִים+נוּ = אֱלֹהֵינוּ, עָשָׂה+נוּ = עָשָׂנוּ,
גֹּרָל+נוּ = גֹּרָלֵנוּ, עַל+נוּ = עָלֵינוּ.

2 מֶלֶךְ+■ִים = מְלָכִים

מִשְׁתַּחֲוֶה+■ִים = מִשְׁתַּחֲוִים, מוֹדֶה+■ִים = מוֹדִים,
כֹּרֵעַ+■ִים = כֹּרְעִים, מָרוֹם+■ִים = מְרוֹמִים.

3 יְקָר+וֹ = יְקָרוֹ

עֹז+וֹ = עֻזּוֹ.

4 גּוֹי+■ֵי = גּוֹיֵי

מֶלֶךְ+■ֵי = מַלְכֵי, גֹּבַהּ+■ֵי = גָּבְהֵי.

WORD BEGINNINGS

1 | הַ+אֶרֶץ=הָאָרֶץ | הַ+אֱלֹהִים=הָאֱלֹהִים, הַ+אֲרָצוֹת=הָאֲרָצוֹת,

הַ+אֲדָמָה=הָאֲדָמָה, הַ+מְלָכִים=הַמְּלָכִים,

הַ+קָדוֹשׁ=הַקָּדוֹשׁ.

2 | וְ+לֹא=וְלֹא | וְ+גוֹרָלֵנוּ=וְגוֹרָלֵנוּ, וְ+יָדַעְתָּ=וְיָדַעְתָּ,

וְ+עַל=וְעַל, וַ+הֲשֵׁבֹתָ=וַהֲשֵׁבֹתָ.

WORD FAMILIES

1 עַל, עָלֵינוּ, מִמַּעַל. כֹּל, כְּכָל, הַכֹּל.

2 אֶרֶץ, הָאֲרָצוֹת. מֶלֶךְ, מַלְכֵי, הַמְּלָכִים.

3 אֱלֹהִים, אֱלֹהֵינוּ.

TEFILLAH PHRASES

1 וְיָדַעְתָּ הַיּוֹם, הוּא אֱלֹהֵינוּ, עָלֵינוּ לְשַׁבֵּחַ, וְלֹא שָׂמָנוּ.

2 אֶל לְבָבֶךָ, בָּרוּךְ הוּא, בַּשָּׁמַיִם מִמַּעַל הוּא אֱלֹהֵינוּ.

3 אֶפֶס זוּלָתוֹ, לְיוֹצֵר בְּרֵאשִׁית, וּמִשְׁתַּחֲוִים וּמוֹדִים.

IT IS FOR US TO PRAISE

The עָלֵינוּ is the closing prayer for all services. The עָלֵינוּ is a declaration of faith in God and is recited while standing.

1. It is our duty to praise the Lord of all,	1 עָלֵינוּ לְשַׁבֵּחַ לַאֲדוֹן הַכֹּל,
2. To declare greatness to the Creator of the beginning,	2 לָתֵת גְּדֻלָּה לְיוֹצֵר בְּרֵאשִׁית,
3. Who has not made us like the other nations of the earth,	3 שֶׁלֹּא עָשָׂנוּ כְּגוֹיֵי הָאֲרָצוֹת,
4. And has not placed us like other families on earth,	4 וְלֹא שָׂמָנוּ כְּמִשְׁפְּחוֹת הָאֲדָמָה,
5. Who has not made our destiny like theirs,	5 שֶׁלֹּא שָׂם חֶלְקֵנוּ כָּהֶם,
6. And our lot the same as other people's.	6 וְגֹרָלֵנוּ כְּכָל הֲמוֹנָם.
7. And we bow,	7 וַאֲנַחְנוּ כּוֹרְעִים,
8. Bend the knee, humble ourselves,	8 וּמִשְׁתַּחֲוִים וּמוֹדִים,
9. Before the Ruler, the Ruler of all Rulers,	9 לִפְנֵי מֶלֶךְ מַלְכֵי הַמְּלָכִים,
10. The blessed Holy One,	10 הַקָּדוֹשׁ בָּרוּךְ הוּא,
11. Who rolled out the heavens and founded the earth.	11 שֶׁהוּא נוֹטֶה שָׁמַיִם וְיוֹסֵד אָרֶץ
12. The seat of God's glory is in the heavens above,	12 וּמוֹשַׁב יְקָרוֹ* בַּשָּׁמַיִם מִמַּעַל
13. And God's powerful abode is in the heights above,	13 וּשְׁכִינַת עֻזּוֹ בְּגָבְהֵי מְרוֹמִים,
14. Adonai is our God, there is no other.	14 הוּא אֱלֹהֵינוּ אֵין עוֹד.
15. Our Ruler is true, all else is nothing,	15 אֱמֶת מַלְכֵּנוּ, אֶפֶס זוּלָתוֹ,
16. As it is written in the Torah:	16 כַּכָּתוּב בְּתוֹרָתוֹ*:
17. And you shall know this day,	17 וְיָדַעְתָּ הַיּוֹם,
18. And bring it into your heart,	18 וַהֲשֵׁבֹתָ אֶל לְבָבֶךָ,
19. Because Adonai is God	19 כִּי יְיָ הוּא הָאֱלֹהִים
20. In the heavens above,	20 בַּשָּׁמַיִם מִמַּעַל,
21. And on the earth below.	21 וְעַל הָאָרֶץ מִתָּחַת.
22. There is no other God!	22 אֵין עוֹד!

***This is only the first part of the עָלֵינוּ prayer.**

עָלֵינוּ לְשַׁבֵּחַ

The עָלֵינוּ prayer proclaims God as the ruler of the world. According to an old tradition, Joshua wrote this hymm as the Israelites crossed the Jordan to enter the Land of Canaan.

In the Middle Ages the עָלֵינוּ prayer was sung by Jewish martyrs as they were led to their deaths. On May 26, 1171, thirty-one Jewish men, women and children in the French city of Blois were burned at the stake. As they marched to their deaths, they defiantly sang the עָלֵינוּ.

HOW TO RECITE THE עָלֵינוּ

When you come to the phrase (7) וַאֲנַחְנוּ כּוֹרְעִים וּמִשְׁתַּחֲוִים you bow at the knees. This indicates your acknowledgement that you are in the presence of the God. There is an ancient tradition of falling to one's knees when the phrase (7) וַאֲנַחְנוּ כּוֹרְעִים וּמִשְׁתַּחֲוִים is recited on Rosh Hashanah and Yom Kippur. Sometimes only the Rabbi and the Cantor kneel and fall.

All I Got Was Words

Nor Verter

When I was a child and fancy free,
my folks had no fine clothes for me.
All I got was words:
Got tsu danken *(Thank God)*
Zoln mir lebn un
zeyn gezunt *(We should live and be well)*

When I was wont to travel far
They didn't provide for me a car.
All I got was words:
Gey gezunt *(Go in health)*
Gey palmelekh *(Go slowly)*
Hob a gliklekhe rayse. *(Have a good trip)*

I wanted to increase my knowledge
But they couldn't send me to college.
All I got was words:
Hob Seykhel *(Have common sense)*
Zey nisht keyn nar *(Don't be a fool)*
Toyreh iz di beste
skhoyre *(Torah is the best merchandise)*

The years have flown,
the world has turned,
things I've gotten, things I've learned,
Yet I remember

Zog dem emes *(Tell the truth)*
Gib tsedukeh *(Give tzedakah)*
Hob rakhomones *(Have compassion)*
Zey a mensch! *(Be a mensch!)*

Un daven mit Kavanah
And pray with
SOUL

Author Unknown